On

of

Seco

Celia Hi

BA(Hons),

Radcliffe Medical Press

Radcliffe Medical Press Ltd
18 Marcham Road, Abingdon, Oxon OX14 1AA

First edition 1993

British Library Cataloguing in Publication Data

A catalogue record for this book is available from the British Library.

ISBN 1 85775 445 X

Typeset by Advance Typesetting Ltd, Long Hanborough, Oxon.
Printed and bound by TJ International Ltd, Padstow, Cornwall

Contents

Preface   vi
How to use this book   viii
About the author   x
Acknowledgements   xi

SECTION 1   THEORY AND PRACTICE

1   Incidence and characteristics of child death   3
    The death of a child is different from other bereavements   5
    Sudden and accidental deaths   7
    Prenatal and perinatal loss   16
    Death from illness   21
    Death from congenital conditions   23
    Socially difficult deaths   27

2   Features of grief and mourning when a child dies   33
    Introduction: starting from experience   33
    The development of bereavement theory   35
    New understandings of grief   42
    What the death of a child means for different
        family members   49
    Mourning rituals   58

SECTION 2   GOOD PRACTICE GUIDELINES

3   Professional roles   65
    Ambulance personnel   66
    Clergy   68
    Counsellors   70
    Funeral directors   73

General practitioners 74
Health visitors 79
Hospital doctors 82
Nurses 86
Midwives 88
Police 91
Registrars of births, marriages and deaths 93
Social workers 95
Teachers 97

4 **Guidelines for all** 100
General principles 100
Supervision 106
Training 109
Skills 111
Helping strategies 112
Resources questionnaire 115

5 **Guidelines for stressful situations** 116
Breaking bad news 116
Emergency procedures and intensive care 120
After the death 123
Attending the funeral 128
On first visiting the family 129
Anniversaries 132
Suicide risk assessment 132

6 **Guidelines for talking with children** 135
Introduction 135
Child experience of loss and bereavement 136
First principles 139
Helping children understand about terminal illness 142
Informing children of the death 143
Telling children about a murder or suicide 146
Summary of dos and don'ts 149

SECTION 3   BEREAVEMENT SUPPORT

7   **Support for families**   153
    Practical support   153
    Befriending   155
    Counselling   158
    Psychology   167
    Psychiatry   168
    Groups   169
    Social activities   172
    Support for children   173

8   **Support for schools**   180
    How schools are affected   180
    Planning and preparation   184
    Psychological support: who does what and when?   188

9   **Support services**   198
    Core conditions   199
    Starting a support group   200
    A co-ordinated approach   204

Appendix A Useful contacts for support organisations   209

Appendix B Children's hospices   215

Appendix C Useful resources for working
    with children and families   219

Essential references   225

Further reading   227

Index   231

Preface

The second edition of this book, published at the start of a new millennium, provides the opportunity to do several things. First, this is an obvious time for updating information and to record the developments which have taken place in support services. Second, recent research which challenges the adequacy of conventional bereavement theory will be called upon to amplify key messages about the needs of families bereaved of a child. Third, the needs of children and youngsters grieving the death of a sibling, playmate or friend, will be given more prominence, with added chapters on guidelines for talking with children and support for schools. Sadly the traumas of Dunblane, Omagh and a host of critical incidents have increased awareness of the needs of children and schools, as well as families.

The authority for writing this book stems originally from the first years of the Alder Centre, founded in 1989. The Alder Centre is situated at the Royal Liverpool Children's NHS Trust Hospital Alder Hey. Its remit is *to support all those affected by the death of a child*, of whatever age and from whatever cause. It recognises that the effects of a child's death extend far beyond the immediate family and includes all those involved in the care of the child before, during and after the death, as well as the wider community. The Centre was initiated by a small group of health professionals in partnership with bereaved parents, and was regarded as a pioneering project. It has since become recognised as a model of good practice nationally and internationally, in providing a multipurpose resource which combines support for bereaved families with training for professionals.

The observations and guidelines offered here are thus grounded in practical experience. Basic learning has been gained by following the first guiding principle which is advocated for professionals offering support: *to listen to what individual people say they want rather than presuming what they need.* The only experts are bereaved family members themselves. Their experiences are quoted in these pages to endorse the core messages that emerge: their need for *understanding, information, choices* and *control.*

This book will give encouragement and reassurance to those who have experience in this field as well as guidance to those who are new to it. Those whose work only rarely brings them into contact with child death may be unsure how to respond. What can they say or do that is helpful, or at least is not going to make things worse? It feels risky to come so close to untimely loss and trauma. How to cope? How will they be affected?

Even those whose work regularly brings them into contact with terminally ill children or bereaved families are vulnerable to feelings of failure and helplessness. Ways of coping have to be found which avoid hard-nosed denial at one extreme, and compassion fatigue at the other.

It is, of course, the nature of grief that makes the front-line professional feel inadequate. Underconfidence can lead to bereaved parents and siblings being referred on for specialist help that may not be appropriate or available. More commonly their needs are overlooked or ignored because it all feels too difficult. Guidelines can provide a useful checklist against experience as well as inexperience, and it is the author's hope that the guidelines offered in this book will build confidence for all.

Celia Hindmarch
May 2000

How to use this book

For most people this is more of a book to dip into than to read from cover to cover. Selected reading may be preferred according to interest and experience. All aspects of child death are covered. Although case examples and statistics relate to the ages 0–19, it is recognised that the child status extends from prebirth to any age while parents are alive to grieve their loss.

There are three sections:

- the first deals with definitions and context, and relates theory to practice
- the second offers good practice guidelines related to various roles, client groups and situations
- and the third section gives an overview of different support services and strategies. The appendices offer information on resources for further support and reading.

It is hoped that all readers will refer to the core messages contained in Chapter 4, *Guidelines for All*. These are simple though not always obvious. The most important ingredient in effective support is, of course, the relationship between the helper and bereaved. Whatever the nature of that relationship, whether health professional/patient, teacher/student, social worker/client, priest/parishioner, as friends or colleagues, common core conditions can be identified which help to create trust. While sensitivity cannot be taught, awareness of the issues can be developed and skills can be practised. The need for adequate support and supervision is strongly emphasised throughout as fundamental to professional good practice in this specially stressful area of bereavement care.

Use of gender

For convenience, references are made to the dead child as male, and to the surviving sibling as female. At the risk of reinforcing stereotypes, adults are referred to in the predominant gender for the role or situation being considered.

About the author

Celia Hindmarch is currently a freelance counsellor and trainer, and part-time tutor on counsellor training courses at Manchester University. She also acts as consultant to Cheshire, Halton and Warrington Education Departments regarding the support given to schools following critical incidents.

She was the first manager and senior counsellor at the Alder Centre bereavement support project, Liverpool.

Acknowledgements

The author is indebted to all those who have contributed directly and indirectly to the book, and in particular to those who have shared their personal experience of grief on the death of a child.

This book is dedicated to all our children.

Section 1

Theory and practice

1 Incidence and characteristics of child death

'We find a place for what we lose. Although we
know that after such a loss the acute stage of mourning
will subside, we also know that we shall remain inconsolable
and will never find a substitute. No matter what may
fill the gap, even if it be filled completely, it
nevertheless remains something else.'

Letters of Sigmund Freud (1961)

When my son Paul was killed in a road accident, a week after
starting his first job, I didn't see that I had anything in common
with younger parents who had lost a baby. But when I have
heard such parents talking in a group 1 recognise the same
pain. I feel so sorry for those parents. At least we had our son
for 19 years.

Dave

Although this book covers many different situations involving
the death of a child, all of them heartbreaking, it is important to
remember that it is now a comparatively rare event in the Western
world. Thankfully, most children recover from their accidents or
illnesses nowadays. Modern healthcare and technology ensure that
most childhood diseases can be cured or controlled.

But some children do die. In 1998, the deaths of children aged
0–19 in England and Wales totalled 9943 (*see* Table 1.1) or 6526
excluding stillbirths (*see* Table 1.2). The impact of child death is out
of all proportion to its incidence, in terms of the number of people
affected and the severity of the effects.

Table 1.1 Number of child deaths (age 0–19 years) by cause in England and Wales 1998

Category of death	Number	%
Sudden and accidental death		
sudden death, cause unknown (inc. SIDS)	250	2.5
road vehicle accidents	487	4.9
other accidents	409	4.1
	1146	11.5
Natal deaths (excluding SIDS)		
stillbirth	3417	34.4
neonatal deaths	2418	24.3
	5835	58.7
Death from illness	2187	22.0
Death from congenital conditions and those arising from birth	568	5.7
Socially difficult deaths		
suicide	110	1.1
murder	45	0.5
drug misuse	52	0.5
	207	2.1
Total of major categories	9943	100

Sources: Series DH2 Mortality statistics: cause
　　　　Series DH3 Mortality statistics: childhood, infant and perinatal
　　　　Health Statistics Quarterly **3**
　　　　Office for National Statistics
Note:　SIDS = sudden infant death syndrome

Table 1.2 Total number of child deaths from all causes in England and Wales 1998

	Under 1 year	1–4 years	5–9 years	10–14 years	15–19 years	0–19 years
Male	2070	413	240	291	875	3889
Female	1555	309	177	189	407	2637
Total	**3625**	**722**	**417**	**480**	**1282**	**6526**

Sources: Series DH2 Mortality statistics: cause
　　　　Office for National Statistics

The death of a child is different from other bereavements

Those who have lost a parent, a spouse and a child will invariably describe their grief for the child as the most painful, enduring and difficult to survive. For emergency services personnel, the death of a child is the casualty they most dread having to deal with. For medical and nursing staff, there is a special sense of failure and frustration when a child dies.

The enduring pain of losing a child cannot be measured, so that it is not possible to say that it is more or less painful to lose a child suddenly or after a long, debilitating illness; nor can it be assumed that the age of the child determines the intensity of the emotions (*see* Figure 1.1). In terms of adjustment, parents of older children have the benefit of more positive memories to draw on, although in another sense they have more to lose, having built up a relationship with the child in its own right.

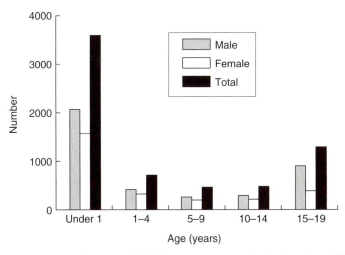

Figure 1.1 Child deaths (age 0–19) from any cause in England and Wales 1998 (excluding stillbirths).

Source: Series DH2 Mortality statistics/Office for National Statistics.

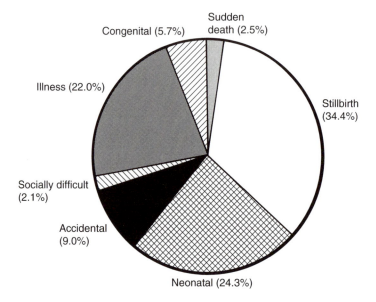

Figure 1.2 Categories of death in children (age 0–19) in England and Wales 1998.

Source: Series DH2 Mortality statistics/Office for National Statistics.

However, it is certainly a different experience, with different factors to be taken into account. The characteristics of various situations will be considered by grouping the deaths into five main categories according to cause and circumstance (*see also* Table 1.1 and Figure 1.2):

- sudden and accidental deaths
- prenatal and perinatal loss
- death from illness
- death from congenital conditions
- socially difficult deaths.

Case studies are included to highlight certain characteristics, with the approval of the families concerned.

Sudden and accidental deaths

Cot death

'Cot death' is the generic term used to describe the sudden, unexpected death of an apparently healthy baby. In about one-third of these cases, the post-mortem discovers an adequate cause to explain the death, such as an overwhelming infection. For the remaining two-thirds, no cause of death can be found and the death is certified as *sudden infant death syndrome* (SIDS). In either case, no-one could have foreseen or prevented the death.

Extensive research has pointed to a number of tenuous coincidental factors for SIDS in both baby and environment, but these are not identified causes. The lack of explanation feeds the mythology associated with this tragic death: Ancient Sumerians believed the baby was stolen by evil spirits; the Bible records a woman's child dying in the night 'because she overlaid it' (1 *Kings* 3:19); some East European countries still routinely record unexplained infant deaths as infanticide.

Facts and figures

Incidence
Variations that occur in the figures for cot death in any given year depend on which definitions are used, the age range, and on what appears on the death certificate. As an approximate guide, the incidence in 1998 for the UK was 0.37 per 1000 live births, accounting for 344 deaths (295 in England and Wales). There has been a significant drop in the rate, estimated by the Foundation for the Study of Infant Deaths at over 60%, since 1991 when the Reduce the Risk campaign was launched. This campaign was based on the identification of certain factors that are *influential* rather than *causal*, and promotes the following advice:

- place your baby on the back to sleep
- cut smoking in pregnancy – fathers too!

- do not let anyone smoke in the same room as your baby
- do not let your baby get too hot
- keep baby's head uncovered – place your baby with feet to the foot of the cot, to prevent wriggling down under the covers
- if your baby is unwell, seek advice promptly.

Age and circumstances
Cot death happens most frequently in the first six months of life, with a peak at two to three months. It is rare in the first month, and the rate drops sharply after six months to become increasingly uncommon in the second year of life. Babies who die suddenly and unexpectedly are typically found dead in their cots in the morning, but some die in the pram, the car, or even in their parents' arms. There are no symptoms, although some babies – perhaps coincidentally – will have had the 'snuffles' in the preceding days.

Males are more at risk than females, as are twins, preterm and low-weight babies. Cot deaths occur in all social classes, although there is a higher incidence among babies born to young mothers, mothers who have a short interpregnancy interval and those who do not present for antenatal care.

Legal procedures

A doctor has to confirm that the baby is dead, either at home or at hospital. As the death is sudden and unexpected, the doctor has by law to inform the coroner, or the procurator fiscal in Scotland. The coroner's officer, or more likely a police officer acting for the coroner, investigates the death by interviewing the parents. The CID may visit if a 999 call has been made. The baby's bedding and clothing are required to be seen and may be removed from the house. The baby is taken to the hospital by police, ambulance officer, doctor or funeral director, for a post-mortem examination to be carried out by a pathologist on the instructions of the coroner. For further information on what happens immediately after a sudden and unexpected death, see the booklet *When a baby dies suddenly and unexpectedly* produced by The Foundation for the Study of Infant Deaths, as part of their useful range of publications (*see* Appendix A).

CASE STUDY

Tom was a bonny nine-pound baby at birth. At seven months he developed a chest infection, which the GP treated with antibiotics. A week later, when Tom seemed fully recovered, the family woke one morning to find him still and lifeless in his cot. Tom's distraught parents, Dave and Sue, knew immediately he was dead, which was confirmed by their GP, who was first on the scene. After prescribing a sedative for Sue, he left with what seemed to the parents like undue haste. They later discovered that he had hurried home to check his seven-month-old baby girl before going to the surgery to look at Tom's notes to see whether he had missed something.

Meanwhile the police had arrived and completed their investigations with sensitivity. Most importantly for Sue, no-one tried to take Tom from her arms until she was ready to let him go. After a brief separation, while Sue and Dave followed Tom in the ambulance (although they wish now they had gone with him) they were reunited at the hospital.

> 'The staff were wonderful', Sue recalls 'A nurse brought Tom in to us holding him close, as if he was still alive, treating him with respect. It meant a lot to us that someone said how beautiful he was, and a couple of the staff sat and cried with us. There was no rush.'

They had to leave Tom for the post-mortem examination over the weekend, but were welcomed whenever they returned to hold him again. Tom was home for two days before the funeral, an important time for the parents and for Tom's six-year-old brother Graeme, who read his book of nursery rhymes to the baby as his way of saying goodbye. Dave and Sue thought it best that three-year-old Michael did not see Tom, but with hindsight now wish they had allowed this, as Michael suffered awful fantasies of what Tom looked like. Fortunately there were photographs to allay his fears.

Sue was left with the overwhelming guilt of knowing that Tom died as she and Dave were sleeping in the same room. 'It took over three years to accept that I couldn't have done anything – and I still find it difficult.'

Death by accident

A major cause of accidental death in children is road traffic accidents (RTAs), where the child may be a pedestrian or passenger, and in later adolescence may be the driver of the vehicle. Other accident situations include death by drowning, choking, burning, falling and poisoning. The death may be immediate or as a result of injuries, and the child's body is likely to be damaged externally, and sometimes severely maimed.

Whether or not other family members are involved in the accident, they will be suffering the effects of trauma. Extreme reactions of shock, disbelief and anger can be frightening and difficult for those in attendance.

Denial and evidence

Denial of what has happened is a natural defence and initially helps the traumatised system to cope. However, if the denial persists, the bereaved person will suffer from extreme anxiety and risks long-term mental health problems. Facing reality requires unambiguous explanation and evidence, and ultimately seeing is believing. The need to view the body or photographs of the deceased has been recorded by those who have worked with the relatives of disaster victims.

These were some of the conclusions reached by Janet Haddington after counselling families who lost a loved one in the sinking of the *Marchioness* in 1989 when, after the first two days, visual identifications of drowned relatives was first discouraged and then disallowed by the coroner's officers:

'The police should understand that identification may not be the sole reason for relatives wishing to view bodies. The bereaved also need to be clearly informed that photographs have been taken and will be made available at any stage in the future should seeing them feel helpful. The bereaved also need to be informed that once the body is released to the funeral director they have the right to view. The manner in which some bereaved have been denied access to view the body has led to long-lasting anger and protracted grief.'

The use of the word 'denied' here is interesting, suggesting that professionals may seek to protect others from pain as a way of denying their own. Sometimes the mother is excluded from seeing the body in the belief that she is not strong enough to cope and may become hysterical.

Legal proceedings

The difficulty of dealing with intense grief reactions is exacerbated by legal proceedings, which may take months or even years to complete. The results of the post-mortem examination may be withheld when parents are anxious to learn every detail about injuries. Accidental death requires a coroner's inquest to establish the cause of death. Where a person has been charged with murder, manslaughter, causing death by reckless driving or infanticide, the inquest is adjourned until the conclusion of the criminal proceedings. The evidence of witnesses and the results of police investigations will not be known until then, leaving parents in an anguish of uncertainty. It helps if the police keep them informed and if the coroner prepares them for the inquest, but too often they feel doubly victimised by an adversarial legal system that excludes them. In the case of a road traffic accident death that leads to a criminal charge and trial, parents desperately want the offender to admit responsibility and show regret. Sadly, the inevitable process of prosecution and defence makes this almost impossible. Most parents seek reparation, not retribution.

However, sentences for convictions of careless, reckless or dangerous driving leave the family and community feeling that a child's life is held cheap. The same applies to amounts paid as compensation. Insensitive or intrusive media coverage will intensify the effects of the trauma.

CASE STUDY

Seventeen-year-old Kevin was a cheerful and popular lad with a sense of fun and adventure. While waiting for the train home one Saturday night, Kevin and his mates explored the goods area of the station and climbed on top of a wagon. Kevin touched the overhead electric wires and was killed outright.

Kevin's mother Betty was called home from her night-shift by the news that Kevin had been involved in an accident. Fearing the worst, she arrived home to find that her husband Kenny had already been taken away by the police. Her telephone enquiries to the local hospitals and police stations all drew a blank, and she was left in an agony of not knowing what had happened. Meanwhile, at the railway station, Kenny was told by the British Transport Police how Kevin had died, and was advised not to see his body. The officer who gave this advice had not seen Kevin himself, but assumed the body to be badly burned. Kenny identified Kevin from his watch and ring.

Back home, Betty's fears were confirmed when one of Kevin's friends who had witnessed the accident returned to his home a few doors away. She was angry and distressed to be separated from Kenny at the time they most needed to be together.

On his return, Kenny told Betty what he knew, and they comforted each other and their daughters as best they could. They struggled with dreadful fantasies of what Kevin looked like and were anxious to know exactly what had happened. Two days after the accident they were shocked to read a tabloid newspaper report of the tragedy prefaced by the headline 'Fried Alive ...'. They were upset to read that British Rail were concerned about the boys trespassing.

Before the funeral, the undertaker heard the tentative note in the parents' question: 'Would you advise us to see him?' He replied that it was up to them, but they might prefer to remember Kevin as he was. They were frightened to do otherwise than heed his advice. Consequently they did not know what they were burying: later, Kenny owned his vision of 'a burnt head of a matchstick'. Betty simply could not believe Kevin was dead. It had all been a ghastly mistake and one day he would just turn up at the back door, having been away on one of his army courses.

At the same time, Betty was inconsolable. She began to resent Kevin's friends and was convinced they were hiding the true story from her. She was advised not to go to the inquest, some four months later, as being 'too upsetting' for her. Kenny attended, and watched helplessly as photographs of Kevin's dead body were passed among the jury – photographs that he did not know existed.

Over three years later, Betty was still angry and bitter. 'I'm left with this void. If I had seen him, I would have known he was dead, instead of waiting for him to come home, which is what I still do.'

Disaster

The deaths of children caught up in a disaster, as at Aberfan, Hillsborough and Lockerbie, awaken themes of violence and sense-lessness. Where there are many deaths together, the intensity of the shared grief is overwhelming, and extremely difficult to resolve. This is compounded by the protracted legal battles to determine responsibility, and it is bitterly resented when no-one is held accountable. Fears of litigation, compensation awards and individual job dismissal make it almost impossible for anyone to show the regret and remorse the parents badly want to hear expressed.

There is usually an overwhelming need to be with others who have experienced or been affected by the disaster. New identities are forged: as casualties, as survivors, as bereaved, as helpers. Multiple losses affect the whole community for many years after the event which has somehow defined its members differently. Gaynor, who survived the Aberfan coal tip disaster which killed her brother and sister, remembers some of the after-effects as follows:

> 'After the disaster the surviving children weren't allowed to play in the street in case it upset other parents. We all felt guilty we were alive. We didn't feel like survivors.'

> (*The Guardian,* 23 March 1999)

A research team is currently investigating the long-term effects of the Aberfan tragedy which claimed the lives of 116 junior school children and 28 adults, mostly teachers, when a slurry tip engulfed the school in October 1966. Gaynor, who was eight at the time, will take part in the study in the hope that its findings will help those affected by the survivors of Dunblane and other tragedies. She has never felt settled in her adult life:

> 'I have always felt insecure and this is the reason I have changed jobs and house so often. It has destroyed a lot of people's lives.

Most of the survivors I know are divorced and have lived very unsettled lives.'

Bombings which have killed innocent children in Northern Ireland, notably at Omagh in 1998, in blatant disregard of the ceasefire, have left lasting scars emotionally as well as physically. Even those bombings which claim no children, as in the Docklands, or which involve no deaths at all, as in Manchester, may affect the security of children who see their homes or schools damaged.

Miraculously only one child and three adults perished as a result of the *Jupiter* sea disaster in 1988, when nearly 400 children embarked on an educational cruise from the port of Piraeus in Greece. Ten years later the trip coordinator has compiled the memories of some of the children and parents. The experience of the ship sinking and the struggle to survive marked the end of a carefree existence for those involved. One parent said: 'I sent away a child and got back a stranger'. An Institute of Psychiatry interim report (1996) found that 52% of 168 *Jupiter* survivors interviewed had experienced symptoms of post-traumatic stress disorder (PTSD); that 14% continued to experience PTSD symptoms for more than five years; that 9% of the group have attempted suicide since the disaster; and that there are significant differences in academic performance compared to contemporaries.

It is important to note also the amazingly strong bonds which can hold people together after disasters, and the inner resources which children can call upon. The *Jupiter* accounts are full of examples of calm self-discipline. When another boat carrying a party of young people hit disaster a year later – the *Marchioness* on the River Thames in London – young friends on the accompanying sister ship *Hurlingham* displayed extraordinary courage in their attempts to save lives.

Prenatal and perinatal loss

Miscarriage

Miscarriage is also known as spontaneous abortion. Nobody knows the true incidence, as many early miscarriages are not reported, but it is estimated that over 20% of all clinically confirmed pregnancies end in miscarriage before 20 weeks' gestation. Allowing for the reality that some women feel relieved to miscarry in the event of an unwanted pregnancy, miscarriage still accounts for the highest incidence of child loss. After the age of viability, set at 24 weeks' gestation in the UK, the fetus is regarded as a baby and its death described as a stillbirth. But for most parents, and particularly for the mother, the growing mass of cells has always been a baby. With the aid of ultrasound scans, parents can now see the growing shape and movements of their baby long before the mother can feel it move inside her.

Early miscarriage means there is nothing to say goodbye to, and no ritual to help make the loss a reality. Anguish and guilt may derive from not knowing what happened to the fetus, which becomes hospital property. Fortunately, growing awareness has enabled health professionals to acknowledge these anxieties. Mothers are now encouraged to see and hold a formed baby, however small, and many chaplains will arrange some kind of funeral long before the law requires it. Most parents will appreciate a scan picture, if one is available, as evidence that their baby existed.

Late miscarriage means the baby has died nearer to a viable age (redefined by the Stillbirth (Definition) Act 1992 as 24 weeks' gestation) and is legally entitled to a funeral. Medical terms such as 'placental insufficiency' and 'cervical incompetence' encourage the mother's feeling that she is to blame. The later the loss, the greater the attachment will have been between mother and baby, and to a lesser extent between father and baby, so that grief reactions are likely to be more intense. The importance of naming the baby, spending time to say goodbye, and a proper and dignified ritual, have all been established as helpful for healthy grieving. Photographs are usually treasured by the parents, and are helpful to other family members such as grandparents and siblings who were not able to see the baby.

CASE STUDY

Faye and Denis always planned to have two children. They hoped for a girl and a boy. Eighteen months after having Michael, Faye lost her second baby, Deborah, at 20 weeks' gestation:

'I was sure she had been dead for a couple of weeks, but at first no-one seemed to take me seriously when I said I knew something was wrong. I didn't even see her, and felt guilty afterwards. I didn't like to ask what happened to her little body, but I guessed. When I went back on the ward nobody knew what to say to me and I couldn't wait to get home.'

Having been told that she might not be able to carry another baby to term, Faye was apprehensive when she became pregnant again eight years later. She lost Jane at 17 weeks, but this was a very different experience.

'Denis came with me for the scan, which confirmed the worst, and he stayed with me when they induced labour. Jane was so tiny she could fit in your hand. We held her and had some photographs taken and the sister asked if we wanted the chaplain to come. We knew she couldn't baptise her but she did a sort of blessing, which meant a lot to us. Jane even had a proper little funeral service, and we can visit the Petal Garden at the local crematorium where the ashes of all premature babies are scattered. I just wish we could have done the same for Deborah.'

Termination

In 1998 the total number of recorded pregnancy terminations in England and Wales was 177 332. Just over 1% of these terminations were medically advised because of fetal abnormality or because the pregnant woman's life was at risk. The vast majority were carried out on the grounds that continuance of the pregnancy would jeopardise the physical or mental health of the pregnant woman or her existing children. (Abortion Statistics 1997, Office for National Statistics.)

Requested termination

Termination as a solution to unwanted pregnancy may be sought for a variety of reasons. In the younger age group, a girl's pregnancy may be at odds with her maturational and educational needs, it may be the result of forced sex or it may be the consequence of trying to get psychological needs met. For an older woman, there may be a conflict with other priorities at that time. She may fear that this baby will impose emotional, mental or physical demands that will be damaging to herself or her family. At any age, she may want the baby but is under pressure from family or partner not to continue with the pregnancy, and may lack the support she needs. Whatever the circumstances, termination is likely to be a negative choice with some level of regret. It may be necessary to deny this conflict of feelings in order to go through with the decision. The medical assessment that follows a request for termination subjects the woman to the kind of scrutiny that is not required of a woman who decides to have a child. Pre-abortion counselling is unlikely to uncover ambivalence or regret in women who do not feel able to make free choices.

Medically advised termination

If there is evidence that a baby will be born with a significant abnormality, either because of a congenital condition or because the baby has been exposed to potential damage, or if the continued pregnancy puts the mother's health at serious risk, then a termination will be offered to the mother. If she decides to terminate on the basis of uncertain risks, she may never know whether the baby would have been all right, and the responsibility of making such a painful decision will weigh heavily. Even when the choice is obvious, the mother is likely to feel guilt and a sense of failure. Again, these feelings may need to be denied at the time in favour of logic and common sense.

The termination of an abnormal fetus is experienced as a double bereavement, compounded by feelings of guilt and inadequacy that the baby was 'faulty'. Whatever the reason for the termination, the feelings of loss may be intense. The grief for what might have been is often underestimated, particularly when the termination has been voluntary and a matter of painful choice.

Stillbirth

In 1998, 3417 stillbirths were registered in England and Wales (*see* Figure 1.1). This figure has risen since 1992, when the Stillbirth (Definition) Act lowered the definition age for stillbirth from 28 to 24 weeks' gestation. There can be few more poignant and distressing experiences than to give birth to a dead baby, or be witness to this cruel loss. The stillness of a new-born baby is a tragic juxtaposition of life and death.

Stillbirths are registered as births and not as deaths. A separate stillbirth form records confidential information that is used only for the preparation of statistics by the registrar general. In the unusual case of a full inquest, a coroner's conclusion will be provided, but is not classified as a verdict because a stillborn baby is deemed not to have lived and therefore there has been no legal death. However, the registration provides an opportunity for confronting the reality and, as such, is a kind of ritual. Parents are issued with a certificate of registration. The Stillbirth and Neonatal Death Society (SANDS) has done much to raise awareness about the need of parents to say goodbye to their baby, and many hospitals now have a room or suite available away from the maternity ward.

Neonatal death

Neonatal means newly-born, and defines the period from birth to 28 days. This overlaps with the term 'perinatal', which applies to the period between the viability time of gestation (24 weeks) and the first seven days after birth, so for that first week the two words can be used synonymously. There were 2418 neonatal deaths in England and Wales in 1998 (*see* Table 1.1). The causes of neonatal death are common to stillbirth: abnormal development, premature delivery and complications during labour. The baby may have been born without the necessary capacity for survival, which is usually anti-cipated before the birth, or unexpected problems during the birth process damage an otherwise healthy baby. In the latter case the mother may be heavily sedated, have undergone an emergency caesarean section, and be quite unwell after the birth. Her own incapacity can have important consequences if the baby dies before she can relate to him.

The baby's initial attachments, however, are to machines and tubes, and the parents' first sight of their baby surrounded by tech-nology and protected by a wall of plastic can be frightening. There is usually an intense longing to hold the baby, which may be frustrated until the baby dies. Neonatal Unit staff encourage parents to handle the baby whenever possible, and share the baby's care. However, it is common for parents to withdraw emotionally and physically from the baby in anticipation of their loss. This can be a source of acute feelings of guilt later on, and is distressing to the staff and other parents on the unit. The loss of a twin, when emotional energies are split between the surviving twin and the dying twin, is specially poignant.

The parents have experienced their baby as having an independ-ent life. That life is valued, however short, and parents will specify hours and minutes when describing their loss. There is often a tragic sense of helplessness, for both parents and staff, as the fight for life is lost. The primary nurse, the consultant and the chaplain may assume great significance for the parents, as being the main characters in the baby's short life.

Death from illness

Malignant disease

The diagnosis of childhood cancer is not the death sentence it is often presumed to be, and the majority of children with the most common form of leukaemia have a good prognosis of long-term survival. Treatments and therapies for cancers and blood disorders are often painful and distressing, involving disfiguring side-effects such as hair loss from chemotherapy and puffy weight gain from steroids. Periods of remission give rise to hope and optimism, but as successive treatments fail for those with a poor prognosis, there is time to prepare for the inevitable outcome.

Some parents and families do plan accordingly, and provide many varied life-experiences for their child's remaining months or years, such as trips abroad and visits to Disneyland. Others do not or cannot even talk about the future and cope by maintaining denial to the end. In either case the question remains whether it is ever possible to feel prepared for the reality of the death when it occurs. Stories are legion of the courage of these children in approaching death. The home services provided by specialist Macmillan nurses and Sargent cancer care workers can help to normalise the family's life and facilitate the child's death at home wherever possible.

CASE STUDY

David was 15 months old when his parents were told the diagnosis to explain a persistent lump (and his mother's intuition) that he was seriously unwell: a stage four neuroblastoma, with a very poor prognosis for recovery. Sue and John remember the compassion of the consultant at their local hospital who was clearly upset to tell them this bad news. David was transferred to the nearest paediatric hospital, Alder Hey in Liverpool, for the specialist treatment he needed. This was one of the worst times: arriving at a strange place at the weekend, when the ward was eerily quiet, and suddenly feeling totally out of control, shocked and angry that this was happening to their child.

Sue's philosophy is to face things head-on, and John's recent experience of losing both parents in an atmosphere of secrecy and denial made them both determined to be open about David's illness. They appreciated the Alder Hey consultant answering their questions honestly, balancing hope with realism. They came to feel part of a team, working together with medical and nursing staff, social worker and play therapist, and became part of a ward culture that enabled parents to support each other.

There followed a regime of chemotherapy, to which David responded well, with a week in hospital and two weeks at home. Sue and John readily responded to the Sargent social worker's advice to include Jane, their three-year-old daughter, in what was going on. As a result, all three of them would sometimes stay with David on the ward at weekends. Otherwise Sue and John took it in turns to be with him while the other maintained a secure base for Jane. Throughout his illness, David's quality of life was high, and they were able to function as a normal family for much of the time. After six months, the time was judged right for surgery to remove the primary tumour. The immediate improvement in David's condition after the operation gave new hope – only to be dashed within weeks when tests confirmed that the cancerous growth had returned. This was the darkest hour for Sue and John, with the realisation that time was running out. After David reacted badly to one last-chance experimental treatment, they felt he had had enough, and active treatment was stopped.

David died at home, without pain, two weeks before his second birthday, hours after watching his favourite Postman Pat videos together with his family. Sue describes it as an extraordinarily peaceful day.

Acute illness

Viral infections such as meningitis can overwhelm a child very quickly. By the time the parents become alarmed by symptoms and call the doctor or take the child to hospital, the child's condition is likely to have worsened rapidly. When the child dies, perhaps within a day or two, the loss is experienced as a sudden death, and the parents are caught in a nightmare of disbelief. Typically parents will blame themselves for not alerting the doctor earlier and so, maybe, reducing the chances of recovery. The mysterious power of an invisible killer disease that can strike without warning lends itself to quite irrational conclusions: parents may become convinced that a playmate was carrying the infection, or that a recent visit to the shops was somehow connected. Fears for the safety of surviving children are likely to run high and lead to overprotective attitudes. The family too may suffer from others' irrational beliefs that it is somehow contaminated by such tragic fortune and thus better avoided.

Death from congenital conditions

Cystic fibrosis

This is the most common genetically inherited life-threatening disorder. However, life-expectancy has increased steadily as symptom treatment has improved; many children with cystic fibrosis now survive into adulthood. Careful exercise and management can sustain a near-normal lifestyle for much of the time.

As the children and parents are in and out of hospital over a number of years, strong attachments form with hospital staff. Hospital and community nurses become part of an extended family, and they come to see the family as friends more than patients. Children who want to talk about their condition may protect their parents from distress by talking to a trusted nurse – perhaps at night when the child is alone and has time to think. The staff are therefore closely involved in the child's life and death.

Heart deformities

Over one-third of hospital child deaths relate to congenital heart conditions, although in a few cases the heart deformity develops as the result of a viral infection. Six children per 1000 are born with some kind of heart abnormality: of these, one-third die soon after birth, and one-third will require surgery. Although the child has had a chronically sick condition, the death is usually experienced as sudden, as most typically occur in surgery and at a young age.

Although the parents are told the risks of survival, the faith required to hand over their child to the surgeon suspends any realistic view. The shock, disbelief and anger that parents experience are compounded by the fatal operation taking place when the child was in the best of health (to optimise the chances of coming through). Thus the parents may have brought in a comparatively healthy child who was skipping down the ward one day, and is dead the next.

One important consequence of this pattern of events is the guilt that parents feel that they were not with their child when he died, and the heavy sense of responsibility that, in consenting to this operation, they virtually signed a death warrant. Anger towards the surgeon and the hospital is often extreme, and more parents are resorting to litigation. This natural anger is overwhelming for

CASE STUDY

New-born baby Clare's feeding difficulties and a blueness around the lips alerted maternity staff that something was badly wrong. John and Maureen, her parents, were told there was a slim chance of her surviving the necessary surgery to insert a shunt. But she did survive, and came through major surgery at 18 months with flying colours. John remembers that they were totally oblivious to the risks at that time – perhaps because they didn't want to know – and had absolute faith in the surgeon.

To all outward appearances Clare grew up a very normal little girl: she went to a normal school, joined the Brownies, Guides and majorettes, and John taught her to swim. But she couldn't run about like other children, and her parents always had to be extra vigilant to make sure she didn't overdo things. And as she got older, the need for more corrective surgery grew with her. 'It was rather like living with a gas leak', John recalls. 'You don't realise the danger until someone comes in from outside and brings it to your notice. We didn't see how much Clare had deteriorated'.

It wasn't until the last year of Clare's life that John and Maureen realised that she might die. Meeting other parents through the Association for Children with Heart Disorders opened their eyes. With no other options left, Clare faced major surgery again at the age of ten-and-a-half years, and this time she did not come through.

'Something inside me just knew she wouldn't make it', says John. 'We really started grieving for her from the time we were told of the operation – like picking up a newspaper dated three months later. But it was still an enormous shock to lose her.'

parents if there is any doubt about the surgeon's competence or assessment of risk, as featured in the Bristol Royal Infirmary inquiry held between 1998 and 1999.

Neurodegenerative disorders

There are literally hundreds of genetically inherited life-threatening diseases, some very rare, which are mostly metabolic in origin. The most common of these conditions include the dystrophies and Batten's disease. The principle feature of these neurodegenerative disorders is the progressive deterioration of the neurological system over weeks, months or years. This often includes a distressing deterioration of mental faculty.

The timing of the diagnosis varies, but typically an apparently well child will develop non-specific symptoms such as epileptic fits, a squint or an awkward gait. At first the degeneration may be slow, and parents can suffer years of struggle and worry, perhaps being labelled as overanxious by the medical profession. As the symptoms increase and the condition worsens, tests lead to a diagnosis. The label makes no difference to the outcome, and the parents will be told that the condition is life-threatening. The bereavement starts here, and some anticipatory grieving will begin as the child's functioning becomes progressively worse.

Parents are desperate to know the prognosis, and most will ask: 'How long has he got?' Time limits and future plans become all-consuming preoccupations. No-one can give a confident prediction of life expectancy, as the progression of the disease can remain on a plateau for several years. Care of the increasingly disabled child becomes the focus of family life, and respite care provides both a lifeline and a potential source of guilt for parents who become physically and emotionally exhausted.

Many of these children die in their early teenage years, usually from an infection which the debilitated system is unable to resist.

After such a death families are vulnerable to wounding remarks such as 'all for the best' and 'blessing in disguise'. Parents lose a lifestyle of care and a social network as well as their beloved child.

Socially difficult deaths

Some deaths carry an element of social stigma, presenting an added difficulty for families coming to terms with their grief. Murder, suicide, deaths associated with anorexia, substance misuse, AIDS, neglect and abuse evoke highly emotive responses at a social level. Such deaths are difficult to talk about, subject to myth and misunderstanding, and reduce the level of sympathetic support forthcoming in other situations. Bereaved families are thus likely to be further isolated.

Murder

The wounds may never heal for parents of murder victims. There may be an agonising period of uncertainty between the discovery that the child is missing and finding the body, then again before the perpetrator is apprehended. If the body is not found, or is mutilated beyond recognition, the reality of the death is hard to reconcile. The legal process then takes over in a way that leaves the family feeling doubly victimised. Sensitive police handling of the case will take into account the importance of the family being kept as fully informed as possible. The parents are tormented by imaginings of their child's final violation, and their private grief is likely to be invaded by the media.

Suicide

Suicide is perhaps the biggest taboo of all, particularly in adolescence. It is hard to accept that a youngster, with all of life's potential before him, should choose to end it. Suicide is a massive rejection of the parents who conceived and nurtured that life. The act of self-destruction, whether or not it was intended to result in death, may well happen at a time when family relationships are fraught and ambivalent.

Denial is an understandable defence against the burden of guilt and sense of failure that threaten to overwhelm the parents. Coroners often collude with this and return an open verdict if at all possible in order to spare the family's feelings. In fact, the uncertainty that follows an open verdict may hinder the grieving. As long as the parents can harbour the belief that there may have been a third party involved, or that an experiment went dreadfully wrong, they will engage all their energies in exploiting every theory that avoids facing reality.

In any case, the experience of social isolation is likely to be the same, adding a sense of shame to the guilt and responsibility. The stresses on parents and siblings are enormous, and suicidal thoughts of joining the dead youngster are commonly experienced. The expression of such dark feelings brings some relief, and contact with other families who have been through this ordeal can be reassuring.

Schools and colleges find it very difficult to deal with the suicide of a student. The events are usually shrouded in mystery and rumour, and a fear of copy-cat actions often prevents the staff from acknowledging the death openly. The myth that talking about suicide encourages others to feel suicidal still persists, while the healthiest outcome is for youngsters to express their feelings of shock and fear. (*See* Chapter 6, pp 146–9)

CASE STUDY

During the last three months of his life Simon had lost his job and written off his first car. In spite of these setbacks he did not appear to be depressed, and his family had no hint beforehand of his suicidal feelings. On a bitterly cold winter day he waited until his mother went out with the dogs, left a note for his parents, took some rope from the loft and made his way to a park behind a nearby pub. There he hanged himself from a tree in an area where he used to play as a child.

By the time the note was found and the police called, Simon's body had been discovered and taken to hospital. At first the

---

police said there was still hope of the paramedics reviving him, when they knew he was dead, which later caused much resentment from the family. There was an agonising two-hour wait before Simon's parents and two older sisters were allowed to go to the hospital. The police were perceived as kind but when they attempted to talk to Simon's father on his own, Simon's mother felt hurt and demanded not to be left out. The family needed to be together and travelled to the hospital in the same car.

At the hospital the doctor who confirmed the death was experienced but cold and detached, and the family wished he had shown some feeling. The family found the nurses to be kind and considerate, and they were given as much time as they wanted with the body. Simon's older sister remembers being upset that his feet were not covered by the sheet.

Waiting for the inquest was a harrowing time, even though the suicide note left no doubt of the verdict. It read: 'Mum and Dad, I did something stupid today. So it is obvious my brain is not right or that I am not right. So I have gone to cure it for good. I love you very much, Simon.' Without any other explanation, the perplexed parents were deeply hurt by unfounded rumours that Simon had been thrown out of home, that he was on drugs, that he had 'got a girl into trouble'. They felt isolated by the implications that his home and family had been inadequate.

Substance misuse

Experimental use of drugs and other substances is widespread amongst young people, and in the UK almost universal as far as alcohol is concerned. The highest risk of accidental death occurs early on in the usage, when youngsters have low tolerance levels and are ignorant about the potentially lethal effects. Of the 52 deaths from drug misuse recorded in England and Wales in 1998 (*see* Table 1.1), it is believed that about one-third died on their first experience. Ambivalent and somewhat hypocritical social attitudes towards drug-taking do not help. Drugs education programmes that aim to minimise risk by giving children the information they need to stay safe are not promoted, on the grounds that such information encourages substance misuse. Parents may find it very difficult to come to terms with their child's behaviour, which was concealed from them, and seek scapegoats to blame. Often the family gets labelled as somehow inadequate.

AIDS

HIV (Human Immunodeficiency Virus) which leads to AIDS (Acquired Immune Deficiency Syndrome) is transmitted through bodily fluids, principally blood, semen and vaginal fluids.

Table 1.3 AIDS cases and deaths in children[1] by exposure category (United Kingdom: cases reported to the end of April 1999)

How children probably acquired the virus	*May 97–Apr 98*		*May 98–Apr 99*		*Jan 82–Apr 99*	
	Diagnosis[2]	*Report[2]*	*Diagnosis[2]*	*Report[2]*	*Total[3]*	*(Deaths)*
Mother to infant	55	60	21	49	332	(143)
Blood factor (e.g. for haemophilia)	–	–	–	–	35	(25)
Blood/tissue transfer (e.g. transfusion)	–	–	–	1	18	(9)
Other/undetermined	1	1	–	–	2	(1)
Total	**56**	**61**	**21**	**50**	**387**	**(178)**

1 Aged 14 years or under when AIDS was first diagnosed.
2 In any given period the number of cases reported may not equal the number diagnosed due to reporting delay.
3 Includes 30 individuals who were aged 15 years or over at the end of April 1999 or at death (6 children infected through mother-to-infant transmission (1 died) 17 haemophilia patients (10 died), and 7 blood recipients (2 died)).

In the case of children being infected with HIV the routes of transmission particular to them are believed to be whilst in the womb, during birth and breast feeding. Also in the UK there are still haemophiliac children who are dying as a result of being infected with the contaminated blood product Factor viii from the USA. There have been no new infections from this route since the mid-1980s.

Obviously a particular feature of these deaths is the anger directed at the hospital for providing the contaminated blood. Alongside the anger is the guilt of all parents who in some way consider themselves responsible, either directly or indirectly, for the infection of their children.

Table 1.4 HIV Infection[1] and deaths[2] in children[3] by exposure category and sex

How children probably acquired the virus	England, Wales and N Ireland			Scotland			Total[4]	(Deaths[2])
	Male	Female	NS	Male	Female	NS		
Mother to infant	268	273	2	18	17	–	578	(151)
Blood factor (e.g. for haemophilia)	263	–	–	17	–	–	280	(105)
Blood/tissue transfer (e.g. transfusion)	17	15	3	2	2	–	39	(14)
Other/undetermined	5	5	1	1	–	–	12	(1)
Total	**553**	**293**	**6**	**38**	**19**	**–**	**909**	**(271)**

1 Includes all children with AIDS, or with virus detected, or with HIV antibody at age 18 months or over.
2 Deaths in HIV-infected children without AIDS are included.
3 Infected when aged 14 years or under.
4 Includes 296 children who were aged 15 years or over at the end of April 1999 or at death (11 children infected through mother-to-infant transmission (1 died), 268 haemophilia patients (91 died), 14 blood recipients (3 died) and 3 in the other/undetermined category).

Data compiled at The Institute of Child Health, London, in collaboration with The Public Health Laboratory Service AIDS Centre.

Such is the stigma still attached to AIDS that most parents of these children are unable to share with others the true nature of their child's condition or cause of death. Sadly the experience of many parents indicates a reluctance by headteachers and governors to accommodate these children in their schools. Against this background, it is all-important to encourage openness between children and parents as the disease progresses.

Care issues and fostering

Deaths that are linked in some way to neglect of the child or to non-accidental injuries evoke strong emotions. They usually take place against a background of deprivation and inadequacy. If the child dies with some real degree of parental responsibility, the parents' grief is likely to be ignored by a society that condemns them. The support of other bereaved parents is not available to them, and expert psychiatric care may be indicated.

Other issues arise with the death of a child who is not in the care of the birth parents. Foster-parents may be excluded from funeral arrangements made by the birth family. The death of a baby born to a girl who is herself in care will have implications for her carers too.

References

Haddington J (1992) Has it really happened? *National Association of Bereavement Services Newsletter.* **8**: 1–5.

Foundation for the Study of Infant Deaths. *When a baby dies suddenly and unexpectedly.*

2 Features of grief and mourning when a child dies

> 'Grief fills the room up of my absent child,
> Lies in his bed, walks up and down with me,
> Puts on his pretty looks, repeats his words,
> Remembers me of all his gracious parts,
> Stuffs out his vacant garments with his form.'
>
> Constance, on the death of her son Arthur
> (*King John* Act III, Scene IV)

Introduction: starting from experience

'When my grandson died, some people thought I shouldn't be grieving the way I was. One person said that losing a child was no different to losing a much-loved partner or parent. I told her that if she ever lost a child or grandchild, to come back and tell me what she thinks then.'   Diane

'Don't talk to me about the grieving process … What a ludicrously inappropriate phrase to define the mental, physical and emotional turmoil you are left to sort out after your child has died.'   Marilyn

Both the grandmother and mother quoted here are expressing their frustration with the way society underestimates their experience of loss. They are saying that the death of a child *is* different from other bereavements, that this difference sets them apart from other people and that bereavement jargon is inadequate to describe the uniqueness of their experience and nature of their grief.

For professionals, too, there are special implications of dealing with the death of a child:

> 'I have had 20 years' experience as an accident and emergency nurse, and I can remember every child we've worked on and lost. I'm never prepared for that. I'm always drained afterwards, emotionally and psychologically. I just want to go home.'   Jan

> 'I've been with the ambulance service over 13 years. Dealing with a child is totally different to an adult, and for me, cot death is more traumatic than anything else. I feel sick and totally useless.'
>
> Ron

Whether personally or professionally involved, the death of a child is seen as the most difficult loss to cope with. It is also seen as the most difficult death to talk about and anticipate. It is important to understand why this is so.

Theoretical concepts are formed in order to make sense of experience. Making sense of experience – of what is thought and felt internally as well as what happens externally – may be very helpful to the bereaved themselves. Equally the search for understanding is driven by professionals asking questions such as: how can bereaved parents and families best be helped by others? When and what kind of intervention is indicated? Who might be most vulnerable?

Models of grief are not dreamed up out of the air. They rely on observation and empirical research, using individual experiences in comparative studies, to create some norms from the similarities and differences which emerge. Thus experience forms theory, and theory informs experience.

However, it is fair to say that conventional theories of grief have been found inadequate when it comes to the death of a child. This is partly due to the fact that the majority of bereavement research studies have concentrated on conjugal grief after the death of a spouse or partner. Perhaps more significantly, these models have rested on some basic assumptions which are now seen to be flawed, or certainly limited by their time. Research developments at the end of the twentieth century challenge these assumptions, and they pay more attention to parental grief and child grief. Alternative and modified models are now available which bring together experience and theory with an exciting freshness, and these will be considered in this chapter. Specifically the concept of the *resolution of grief* will be challenged.

First, the features of grief and mourning which have traditionally established our norms will be summarised, before questioning how those norms apply when a child dies.

The development of bereavement theory

Bereavement has come to mean the loss by death of someone significant, although it originally referred to the marauding practices of bands of reavers many centuries ago, raiding the livestock of neighbouring clans. Thus, to be be-reaved implies being robbed or deprived of something or someone of value, so that one is necessarily poorer for the loss. To be deprived of someone of value implies attachment, and the degree of attachment will determine the degree of loss experienced, which leads to grief:

- *bereavement* is what happens
- *grief* is what one feels in reaction to the bereavement
- *mourning* is what one does to express grief.

The twentieth century, Western understanding of grief maintains that successful mourning means that the bereaved must disengage from the deceased. Continued attachment to the dead person is seen as denying the reality of the loss. This notion is traced to Freud (1917), with quotations such as the following to support it: 'When the work of mourning is completed the ego becomes free and uninhibited again'; and 'Mourning has quite a precise psychical task to perform: its function is to detach the survivor's hopes and memories from the dead.'

The British psychiatrist John Bowlby said that the important focus for understanding grief is what happens when attachments are threatened or broken, i.e. strong emotional reactions occur automatically (Bowlby, 1969–80). When faced with loss, attachment behaviour is activated as a chain reaction of distress, anger and withdrawal, all geared towards retrieving the loss. This forms the pattern of the grieving process.

Bowlby's ideas about grief were consolidated and developed by another British psychiatrist, Colin Murray Parkes, via extensive studies of widows in the 1970s. Grief became increasingly understood as a predictable set of behaviours in response to the environment, and resolution of the grief was seen as getting through these reactions to the point where the attachment was dissolved and the reality of the loss finally accepted. These grief reactions have been variously described as parts or stages of a process, though Parkes himself prefers the concept of *phases*, and describes four phases of mourning (Parkes, 1972; Parkes and Brown, 1972).

The American psychologist William Worden, whose book *Grief Counselling and Grief Therapy* (1991) is widely regarded as a standard text, adds to this model the concept of *tasks* of mourning which relate to each of the phases. These four phases, with their associated features and tasks, are summarised in Table 2.1.

Table 2.1 The four phases of grief

Phase	Features	Task
1 Denial	Shock, disbelief, sense of unreality	To accept the reality of the loss
2 Pain/distress	Hurt, anger, guilt, worthlessness, searching	To experience the pain of grief
3 Realisation	Depression, apathy, fantasy	To adjust to life without the deceased
4 Adjustment	Readiness to engage in new activities and relationships	To relocate emotional energy elsewhere

Worden's emphasis on the tasks of mourning encourages both mourner and helper to recognise the potential for aiding the grief work in hand. At the same time the idea of task suggests a necessary degree of resolution before the next phase can be negotiated and the whole process can be successfully completed. However, Worden takes care to point out that many variable factors will influence an individual's progress through these phases, and that their culmination will not restore the mourner to a pre-grief state. It is also important to note that in the second edition of his book, Worden revises Task 4 from 'withdraw emotional energy from the deceased and reinvest it in another relationship' to 'emotionally relocate the deceased and move on with life'. In particular, he takes into account here the difficulty bereaved parents have with the notion of emotional withdrawal from their children. In asking When is mourning finished? Worden seeks to acknowledge the ambiguity of the question while maintaining that there is such a thing as 'a completed grief reaction'.

When tasks of mourning are not completed, we are led inevitably to the notion of 'abnormal' grief reactions. Such a label relates to the medical model of grief which measures reactions as 'healthy' or 'pathological'. Nonconformity with behavioural norms is seen as denial of reality.

So, taking care to avoid such unhelpful language, we attempt to summarise the conventional view of predictable grief reactions, and what happens when they differ from the norm.

Predictable grief reactions

These are defined by Worden as both clinically predictable and common across the whole spectrum of the grieving experience. A broad range of feelings, sensations, thoughts and behaviours fall within this description, including:

- feelings of numbness, sadness, anger, guilt, anxiety, despair, loneliness, powerlessness, yearning, freedom, relief

- physical sensations of shock, fatigue, hollow stomach, aching limbs, dry mouth, breathlessness, tightness in the throat and chest, sensitivity to noise
- thoughts of disbelief, confusion, disorientation, obsessional pre-occupation with the deceased, visual and auditory hallucinations
- behaviours such as sleep disturbance, lack of appetite, absent-mindedness, crying, sighing, restless overactivity, searching, calling out, lethargy, dreams, visiting the grave and special places, treasuring reminders and avoiding reminders.

It is important to note that although the intensity of these reactions can be alarming, both for the bereaved person and to those around, they can all be regarded as appropriate responses. It is often the duration of the response which calls it into question as 'usual'.

Complicated grief

This is the umbrella term to describe reactions which differ from the norm, with negative consequences. Complicated grief may mean simply that the circumstances are complicated (*see* below) or some-times the phrase is used as a euphemism for 'failure to grieve', with all that implies.

There are various classifications of complicated mourning. Each of these classifications suggests a denial of some aspects of the loss, or implies a frustrated state of trying to hold on to the lost relationship.

- *Inhibited or delayed grief* denotes an inability to mourn and an avoidance of the painful feelings. For some reason the bereaved person is unable to accept the reality of the loss.
- *Distorted bereavement* describes an exaggerated aspect of grieving, commonly anger or guilt, which prevents the expression of other feelings such as sorrow and yearning. This is often linked to the sense of desertion when the relationship with the deceased was a very dependent one.

- *Chronic grief* is recognised in those who continue to grieve intensely and unremittingly long after the event. The bereaved person remains acutely distressed in a way that seems inappropriate and disabling. There is continued crying, anger and idealisation of the loved one.

Depression is often associated with the denial or avoidance of painful feelings. Typically the depressed mourner experiences fatigue, loss of libido, irritability and perhaps suicidal impulses. For some, the painful feelings threaten to be so overwhelming that a high anxiety state is produced. Panic attacks and phobias may be associated reactions. Grief may be acted out in behaviours which then become problematic in themselves, like alcohol or drug dependency, inappropriate sexual behaviour and eating disorders. Displaced pain may be experienced psychosomatically as a physical ailment without any discernible cause.

Why do some people experience grief as more difficult, more complicated, more disabling than others? Commonly identified factors are grouped by Worden in four categories.

1 *Relationships.* Relationships which are seen as difficult to grieve include ambivalent relationships, such as love/hate; highly dependent relationships; relationships with a strong degree of identification; abusive relationships; 'unfinished business' between the deceased and the bereaved.
2 *Circumstances.* Certain circumstances in themselves preclude any working through of grief reactions, such as the 'missing, presumed dead' scenario; the lack of an identifiable body; bizarre or uncertain cause of death; a situation involving multiple losses, perhaps including injury to the bereaved.
3 *Personal factors.* These may relate to a history of difficult losses, or early parenting difficulties. Some are seen as vulnerable because they do not cope well with any stress; and others for the opposite reason, that they are stress-resistant. This latter group may be busy helping others and find it hard to recognise their own needs.

4 *Social factors.* An individual's reactions to loss will in some degree be dependent on the reactions of family, friends and the wider community. Any socially unacceptable grief that carries a stigma, such as termination, AIDS-related death or suicide, limits the amount of support available and increases isolation. The absence of a support system is seen as a key indicator of problematic grieving.

Conventional theory applied to the death of a child

How do the above norms apply to the death of a child? To begin with, most of the factors which are identified as indicators of complicated grieving apply to bereaved parents as a matter of course.

- *Relationships* between children and parents are necessarily dependent, usually with a high degree of identification, and are often ambivalent. And the business of parenting is always unfinished.
- *Circumstances* of child death are always traumatic in the sense of being unnatural and unusual, and often they are traumatic in the sense of being sudden and bizarre.
- *Personal factors* which inhibit grief may have more to do with the parents' need to care for their other children, or new babies, than personality traits.
- *Socially*, bereaved parents learn that the death of a child *per se* is embarrassing to the majority of people.

In terms of grief reactions, these are seen to be more extreme. For example, suicidal thoughts and feelings are common to bereaved parents. It is quite usual for parents to keep the (child's) room unchanged and the (child's) clothes unwashed for a much longer period than would be considered usual in other bereavements. Too often the intensity and chronic nature of the grief reactions of bereaved parents attract labels such as pathological, abnormal or unhealthy.

Those who provide support may have unrealistic expectations about the capacity of bereaved parents to resolve their grief. A revealing questionnaire conducted by the Alder Centre in Liverpool in 1991 showed that professionals and non-bereaved volunteers had a more optimistic view of outcome than either the bereaved parents they were supporting or parent volunteers.

The features of grieving for a child thus establish a different set of norms. Does that mean that grieving parents are by definition seen as a sub-group outside the mainstream, as destined to experience problematic grieving, and therefore incapable of achieving a resolution of their grief?

Resolution of grief is a difficult concept for parents. Many would reject the idea that grieving for one's child can ever end, and some consciously choose to stay with the intensity of their early grief as a mark of loyalty to the child they can no longer care for. The saying 'time heals' holds a hollow promise for John, whose 10-year-old daughter Clare died during a heart operation, and who speaks here for a significant proportion of bereaved parents:

'When newcomers join us at the Centre, they remind us all of how we were not so long ago, and for me that's good. I don't ever want to leave that behind. I want to always be reminded of the intensity of what I felt, and time robs you of that.'

The concept of enduring grief is one that seems entirely appropriate to parents whose prime task is to keep alive the memory and meaning of their child's life. Marking anniversaries, birthdays and holding a picture of the child's would-have-been development, are ways of continuing a lifelong duty of care.

Peppers and Knapp (1980) coined the phrase 'shadow grief' to describe the burden of grief that mothers of children who died in infancy carry for the rest of their lives. The shadow may cast a black pall at significant times, but is always in the background as an aching reminder of the qualified joy of giving life. For some, this 'shadow grief' may recede with time, but for most parents this sense of enduring sorrow is both natural and normal.

Clearly, the conventional theories which look towards the resolution of grief are inadequate when applied to the death of a child.

New understandings of grief

During the 1990s the field of bereavement theory has been illuminated by a multidisciplinary, international group of researchers who are said to represent a post-modernist view of grief. Writers such as Margaret and Wolfgang Stroebe from Holland, Mary and Kenneth Gergen, Robert Hansson, Dennis Klass, Phyllis Silverman, and Steven Nickman from the USA and Simon Rubin from Israel, have challenged the dominant twentieth century models as needing expansion and revision. These challenges are particularly helpful for our understanding of parental grief.

In 1992 Stroebe and Gergen published a ground-breaking article entitled *Broken hearts or broken bonds* which questioned the prevailing view that good adjustment to bereavement is seen as the breaking of ties between the bereaved and the deceased. They pointed out that historically this was not always so, as reflected in nineteenth century English literature. The more romantic notion of love and death in Victorian times viewed the breaking of bonds as destroying identity and the meaning of life.

Twentieth century psychology, by contrast, has encouraged goal-orientated behaviour, and has valued efficiency, rationality, independence and autonomy. Applied to grief, debilitating responses are seen as problematical until worked through to the restoration of normal functioning. The idea of 'letting go' is commonly seen as desirable and necessary for building a new identity. Consequently the principles of grief counselling have followed the view that the bereaved person has to be helped to give up their attachment to the dead; or conversely, those who persist in retaining bonds with the dead are seen as in need of counselling.

If bereavement theory is subject to the historical perspective in the Western world, it is further challenged by a comparison with grief in other cultures. Japanese rituals, for example, encourage continued contact with the deceased. The placing of food on the altar dedicated to a loved one is regarded as normal practice in Japan. This provides an interesting contrast with the buying of a birthday cake for a dead child and how that would be viewed in the West.

Stroebe and Gergen conclude their article by arguing for:

'... an appreciative understanding of grief in all its varieties ... that there are many goals that can be set, many ways to feel, and no set series of stages ... that many forms of expression and behavioural patterns are acceptable reactions to loss.'

By 1996 Klass and Silverman continue and strengthen the argument for respecting the importance of *continuing bonds* in their introduction to the book carrying these words as the title. They point out that the prevailing twentieth century models of grief not only contained cultural assumptions which valued disengagement as the goal of mourning, but they also overlooked some important evidence to make the theory fit. This took the form of research findings about the experience of surviving spouses having an ongoing sense of the dead partner, which was seen as a denial of the reality of the loss. Changes in adoption practices are also quoted as challenging the conventional view that it is not possible to be involved with more than one attachment at a time.

'To insist on a separateness that keeps very clear boundaries between people requires a view of human functioning that fails to appreciate the importance of connection and relationship.'

Klass and Silverman argue that an ongoing sense of relationship is both natural and normative. An inner representation of the dead person replaces the living reality without denying the loss. The task of relocating the deceased, as described by Worden, is about accommodating a relationship which is different and which changes over time. The other contributors to *Continuing Bonds* consider different aspects of bereavement but have a consistent message for the reader:

> '... that the resolution of grief involves continuing bonds that survivors maintain with the deceased and that these continuing bonds can be a healthy part of the survivor's ongoing life.'

Now the challenge for those who support the bereaved is about how to help them hold and adapt the continuing relationship in a new way, rather than to separate from it.

Another significant contribution to these fresh understandings of grief comes from Simon Rubin and his research studies of Israeli parents who lost adult sons in the Yom Kippur war of 1973 and in the Lebanon conflict of 1982. These studies took place in 1986, four and 13 years respectively after bereavement (in Klass and Silverman, 1996).

Rubin argues that the outcome to child bereavement relates to two different processes. One is functional, that is, how the parent responds to the traumatic loss on biological, psychological and social levels. The other is about relationship, how the parent has internalised and reorganised the continuing relationship with the dead child. Conventionally, outcome measures have concentrated on levels of functioning alone, linked to observable data on medication, time off work etc. Rubin's 'Two-Track Model of Bereavement', as he calls it, allows for the significance of how the internalised relationship affects the parent and the whole family.

The data relating to this second area (Track 2) reveal some interesting observations from the studies involving Israeli parents:

- parents evaluated their dead sons more favourably than their living sons
- parents evaluated their dead sons more favourably than they did themselves

- the dead sons were viewed as somehow closer and more access-ible than the living
- the passing of time resulted in parents feeling more involved with the image of the deceased, not less – this was in contrast to the way that dysfunctional symptoms (Track 1) decreased over time.

Rubin concludes that:

> '... continuing involvement with the deceased is to be expected. It is how the involvement is maintained, and at what and whose cost, that becomes the important question.'

Implications for bereaved parents – and some alternative models of grief

These shifting perspectives generally offer a more flexible and positive understanding of parental experience of enduring grief. The fact that *the death of a child is forever* (the title of Rubin's chapter in *Handbook of Bereavement*, Stroebe *et al.*, 1993) is validated. Specifically, Rubin's observations direct our attention to how con-tinuing bonds can be respected and accommodated in a way which minimises any damaging effects on the family as a result of the child's death.

When the reality of the continuing relationship between parent and child beyond the grave is recognised socially, the parent is better able to adapt to the internalised representation of the child. They can grow and age together.

> 'The end of grief is not severing the bond with the dead child, but integrating the child into the parent's life and into the parent's social networks in a different way than when the child was alive.'

(Klass, 1996)

Social support is therefore crucial to how bereaved parents can cope and live with their loss. This kind of support is nowhere better demonstrated than in the self-help organisation for bereaved parents, The Compassionate Friends (TCF). They have developed a language which translates bereavement theory according to their own experience of the bereavement journey.

The TCF model

Within The Compassionate Friends' own terms of reference, the course of grief is defined as follows:

- *Newly bereaved*. This stage represents the tension between reality of loss and a sense of a future together despite the separation. Linking objects may capture this tension, such as treasured toys, clothes and photographs. Socially, parents will hope that family and friends will not expect them to snap out of their grief after weeks or months.
- *Into their grief*. Identity seems to be an important issue at this stage, as parents have to re-assess their relation to work and family life. Marriages may experience conflict as both partners seek to find their own best ways of coping with overwhelming feelings. Or perhaps one parent will associate with one aspect of the child, while the other parent holds another aspect. Socially, for members of TCF, shared understanding can lead to more confident communication of needs to the wider community.
- *Well along in their grief*. Here the tension is between letting go and holding on. The tension may be to do with feelings such as guilt or anger, or it may relate directly to the image of the child and what that image means. Memories move with the present. Socially, the meaning of present and future is connected to one's identity as a bereaved parent.
- *Resolved as much as it will be*. Grief does not abate, but it changes. Looking back, there is a sense of difference. The transformation of the inner bonds with the dead child is complex but eventually,

hopefully, can be part of ongoing life, helping to make meaning rather than destroy it. Socially, there may be a desire to make sense of this pain, to work for others' benefit, to make a difference. In TCF, as well as in the wider community, parents can find a developing bond with their child through new developments in their own lives – as a parent to a new child, as a fundraiser or a befriender.

Whirlpool of grief

This model of parental experience of grief comes from the work of Dr Richard Wilson, a consultant paediatrician at Kingston Hospital who has worked closely with bereaved parents who lost a child through SIDS (Sudden Infant Death Syndrome). Back in the 1980s, he was aware that conventional models of grief with their stages and phases did not sufficiently take into account the experience of families he knew. The alternative model he constructed has been well received by parents trying to make sense of their experience.

The model depicts an unsuspecting oarsman rowing along the 'River of Life' who is suddenly plunged down the 'Waterfall of Bereavement' to the 'Whirlpool of Grief' below. The whirlpool carries one round and round, visiting the same emotions time and again, with the occasional respite in the shallows and the risk of being cast against the rocks. The time spent in this period of disorganisation will vary, and some who have been washed up on a bank will choose to stay there. But when the time is right for reorganisation, the 'River of Life' leads away from the whirlpool to calmer waters (*see* Figure 2.1).

Those who have come across this analogy have found it a helpful and attractively simple model. These are Richard Wilson's comments about it:

'It may be a little fanciful. However, it is less rigid than sug- gesting that there are stages of grief which must be completed. People cannot be healed by shepherding them through a fixed

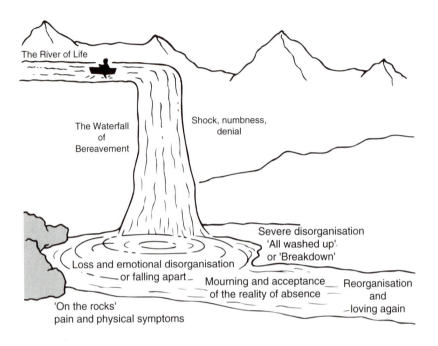

The River of Life

The Waterfall
of
Bereavement

Shock, numbness,
denial

Severe disorganisation
'All washed up'
or 'Breakdown'

Loss and emotional disorganisation
or falling apart

Mourning and acceptance
of the reality of absence

Reorganisation
and
loving again

'On the rocks'
pain and physical symptoms

Figure 2.1 The whirlpool of grief.

treatment plan; however, we may be of some assistance as they make their way along their own difficult and personal journey.

Grief is a turbulent time, and although there may be precious periods of calm, violent emotions which had seemed to be over can return. They are innumerable and all valid. In grief there is a disorganisation of life and thought and values, but most people are then able to reorganise their life in a new way. Although old emotions can always return in almost the same intensity, they do so less frequently and for shorter periods of time.'

The value of this model is that it emphasises the need to listen to parents rather than rely on a taught framework. Bereavement support requires skill and sensitivity rather than knowledge.

Normalisation

This is a word which has gained usage since its association with reactions to trauma. Frank Parkinson has coined a phrase which is often quoted in defining post-traumatic stress reactions:

'The normal reactions of normal people to events which, for them, are unusual or abnormal.'

(Parkinson, 1993)

The emphasis here is on the event, rather than categorising personal reactions to the event. This positive re-framing is the reverse image of the previous tendency to pathologise unusual grief reactions. Normalising those responses which threaten to set people apart can be very reassuring.

What the death of a child means for different family members

Parents

As noted above, the grieving of parents may become 'as resolved as much as it will be', but will never be over and done with. Parents suffer multiple losses when their child dies. Obviously the primary loss relates to the attachment and dependency of a unique individual, while the absence of a child represents much more. Parents will also be grieving other losses:

- part of their own sense of self, physically, emotionally and spiritually
- their connection to the future
- unfulfilled expectations and ambitions
- some of their own treasured qualities and talents
- a source of love and acceptance

- a sense of power and control over what happens to them
- social status and social contacts.

The loss of a child is perceived as different to other griefs. As one parent put it:

> 'When you lose your parents, you lose your past; when you lose a child, you lose your future.'

The relationship between parents will be tested, and the whole family system will be stressed. For many mothers there is a particular threat to identity when a child dies. For many fathers, the death of a child is a real assault on their essential role as provider and protector.

Age of the parent

Research seems to indicate that younger parents seem better able to adapt to the loss of a child, while older parents appear to be less capable of recovering from the extreme chaos of the experience (Stroebe *et al.*, 1993).

Age of the child

The age of the child is a principal factor in the significance of the loss, although the death of a child at any age is untimely. A preterm or newborn baby has a fantasy existence for the parents and remains a dream-child in death. A baby who dies within the first year of life leaves the aching arms of a mother from whom he has hardly separated physically. At this age bonding with both parents (or principal carers) is likely to be at its most intense.

As the young child develops, so does its place in the family. Again, a first child will become central to the parents' emotional life. Sometimes a child takes on a special significance for one of the parents: a mother may feel that a particular child 'belongs' to her, or a father may identify strongly with one child as meeting his own needs. As the child becomes more of a real person, developing a separate identity, relationships become more complex. Ambivalent feelings and conflict inevitably affect the child–parent relationship in the teenage years. As one of the tasks of adolescence is to separate from parents and achieve independence, the death of a teenager is likely to leave in its wake a complicated web of unresolved feelings.

Effect on parents

Effects on the individual parent will obviously vary according to the quality of the relationship with the child, personality, previous experience of loss and what kind of support is available. Parents are often affected by doubts of their sanity and their worth.

- 'Am I going mad?' is a usual response to the extreme distress and disorganisation of the early months of mourning.
- 'Can I go on?' is a usual response to the feelings of worthlessness and despair that make it hard to face another day.
- 'I'd like to join him' is a usual response to feelings that the child has deserted the parent, and the parent has failed the child.

The parenting role

Effects on the parenting role will obviously be dramatic when an only child dies. In the eyes of society, they are no longer parents, no longer a family. The direct line of genetic descent has come to an end. Where there are other children, parental grief is likely to be inhibited and tempered by their needs, which may cause resentment or relief. When the surviving children are young, or when other pregnancies quickly follow the bereavement, mothers in particular do not have the space and time to themselves to grieve and are vulnerable to depression. On the other hand, parents who find they can think only of the dead child have little interest or energy for their other children. They may be aware of this and feel guilty about it but it takes a huge effort to do otherwise. Women whose entire identity and self-esteem depend on motherhood may lose a vital sense of self, suffer chronic guilt and face a huge task of adjustment.

Fathers who see themselves as the family provider and protector will feel they have failed in their responsibility, and this may threaten their sense of manhood.

The marriage or partnership

Effects on the marriage or partnership will depend largely on the strength of the couple's relationship beforehand. Any needs that are not being met will be magnified by the loss and cause resentment, particularly if the child supplied some of those needs for one or other of the parents. Initially, a reasonably open and trusting relationship will allow the parents to comfort each other, although as time goes on even the closest of couples find that grief separates them in some way – it is essentially a lonely experience. Two people cannot grieve at the same pace nor tend to each other's needs without sacrificing their own. One father put it this way: 'It's like both of you having flu at the same time. You feel so wretched that you can't help your partner.'

Another major factor is the different ways in which the partners may express their grief. Stereotypically, the mother copes with her pain by crying and talking, while the father copes with his pain by being active and busy. These differences may be respected, but are more likely to cause resentment that the husband does not appear to be grieving or that the wife is draining him emotionally. They may turn to others for understanding and thus widen the rift. However it happens, a significant number of bereaved couples end up living separately, and most couples experience severe strains on their relationship. An Australian study by Nixon and Pearn (1977) found that marital breakdown occurred in 24% of families following the drowning of a child.

Dot, whose only child Christine died from cystic fibrosis, reflects here on how she and her husband grew apart after Christine's death:

'Bob and I started by grieving together, but after those first two weeks in the depths of despair we couldn't keep in step. I'd look across at him and think, "He's not thinking about Christine at this moment, and so if I say something now, I will be invading his peace … let him have this break". But then as time went on, I realised that I could cope with my own very mixed emotions. In a way I was happier not to have to share them. I suppose in my own way I was shutting other people out, including Bob, but somehow that felt safer to me. I think that was the trigger point for grieving apart. Bob then threw himself into his work, and I was left to pick up the pieces of my life, and so our different ways of coping took us further apart. I think grief is such an individual thing that I don't believe you can grieve as a couple.'

John and Sue, whose second child David died of cancer, also found that they grieved in separate ways, but found a way of communicating their needs which strengthened their relationship. John explains:

'A major factor which helped to bind us together was our relationship with our daughter, Jane. Answering the questions of a three-year-old forced us to bring things out in the open for ourselves.'

Grandparents

Grandparents have an acute sense of broken continuity in the fabric of their own family as well as grieving the loss of the individual child. The effects of losing a grandchild are often underestimated. The two-generation gap can free grandparents to indulge the child with the kind of attention and affection which creates a special bond between them. Grandchildren represent a continuing link with the future at a time of life when one is increasingly aware of one's own mortality. Grandparenting presents another opportunity to endow children with hopes and expectations, although often tempered by a more realistic view and more tolerant attitudes.

Some grandparents will have been involved directly with the care of the child, particularly when both parents are in employment outside the home or when a young mother is still living at home. In these cases the grandparent takes on a parenting role and the intensity of grief is more akin to that of the parent. Grandparents are also likely to be closely involved with the support of both child and parents in the case of terminal illness.

It is this dual role and relationship that causes most anguish to grandparents. They suffer their own grief, and are affected deeply by their own child's grief. They often feel helpless and inadequate in the support they can offer, frustrated by their inability to comfort and protect. This was Diane's experience:

'Other people feel I shouldn't be grieving the way I am, because Anthony was only a grandson. We weren't just nanna and grandson, we were friends. In my case, I'm grieving not only for Anthony but for my daughter as well. I found I couldn't help her.'

Siblings

Brothers and sisters have been called 'the forgotten mourners'. Sadly, their own grief reactions are often overlooked. Older siblings may be encouraged to 'be strong' for their parents. The effects of sibling loss on young children are not easily remembered or understood, and their needs are not always expressed directly. The age and developmental stage of the grieving child is an important factor, of course, but before looking at different age groups, what are the common factors affecting all siblings?

First, there is the parents' grief and the ways in which their reactions affect their other children. What happens at the time of the death and what the surviving children are told are both crucially important. At any age, a child will be affected by the parent's distress and made anxious by upheaval in the home and family. There is a natural inclination to protect children from witnessing their parents' grief. Yet it is essential for them to see their parents mourn, or they will believe that the dead child was not loved and fear that they would not be mourned either if they were to die.

Siblings are also affected by the impact on the family as a system and the balance of relationships within it. All are required to adjust to the void left by the dead child. One consequence may be that a surviving sibling 'takes the place' of the dead child, fulfilling a particular role with regard to one or both of the parents. Another possible outcome, in a situation where the dead child was intensely idealised by the parents, is that a sibling can become the scapegoat for parental anger and guilt. She finds herself competing with an angel, and is found wanting. Families that normally function by sharing feelings and being open about difficulties will obviously fare better than those that avoid emotions. Families that already have disordered patterns and a history of conflict may be plunged into chaos by the traumatic loss of a child, with serious consequences for all family members.

At any age, siblings lose an ally, particularly when left as an only child. Sibling relationships tend to be ambivalent, with love and affection interwoven with resentment and rivalry. Whatever that balance, the sibling loses a playmate or companion, and someone to identify with in the generation struggle with the adult world. For twins and siblings of a similar age the natural bond is closer. Older siblings are likely to be left with feelings of responsibility and maybe irrational guilt that they could not protect their younger brother or sister. Younger siblings are left with a feeling of insecurity following the failure of their older brother or sister to pave the way to adulthood successfully.

Ages and stages

The age of the sibling is seen as the key factor in anticipating the child's experience of grief, and so provides guidance as to what to say and do. Often, the adults involved will be wary of exposing a young child to information or experiences which she is assumed to be 'too young to understand'. Before going on to describe the features relevant to age groups, it is important to note that children do not automatically reach a new level of understanding on a birthday!

Children mature at different rates, and any significant loss may cause regression to a previous stage of development: for example, an eight-year-old will cling to mother again like a four-year-old. It is also helpful to remember that knowledge comes through experience: what a child understands depends more on her previous experience of the world than on her age.

A word of caution about how adults perceive children, because the way we communicate our understanding is determined by the level of language we use. Children are exposed to images of death, via the media and religious symbolism, long before they have the words to describe them. Therefore the tendency is always to underestimate what a child can understand. At the same time, a child's emotional immaturity restricts the ability to cope with intense distress for long periods. This leads to the tendency to underestimate the effects of the bereavement. (*See* Chapter 6 *Guidelines on talking with children* for more on ages and stages.)

Most common anxieties for siblings

Across the board, the most common anxieties of siblings can be crudely summarised as:

- 'Did I cause it?'
- 'Will I die too?'
- 'Who now cares for me?'

It follows that key needs for siblings are information, reassurance and attention. It is important to remember that the complex effects of the *secondary losses* experienced by siblings, such as the loss of normality and parental attention, can be more traumatic than the bereavement itself.

Concept of enduring grief for siblings

Karen's sister died suddenly when she was 10 and Karen was six years old. Now in her mid-thirties, Karen continues to miss Elaine at a deep level:

'All the important events in my life that have taken place have never been complete because there is always someone missing. My wedding was difficult for me as Elaine would have been my bridesmaid and totally involved in the preparations. Then there have been the births of my two children – I had no big sister to share these wonderful moments with. It just seems to get harder and harder as time goes by. I also struggle with my emotions if my children are ill, though I put a brave face on to everyone. I live in constant fear that they will be taken away from me, and I know this fear will never leave me until I go to my grave.'

What helps?

The following are commonly identified as being helpful to siblings, with the benefit of hindsight:

- being told what was happening
- being involved, especially going to the funeral
- thinking and talking about my loss
- meeting other children who have lost a brother or sister
- talking to someone outside the family – someone who shows care and understanding without being intrusive.

This last point is illustrated by Rebecca, who was 19 when her sister Anna died suddenly aged 15:

'I really did appreciate the concern shown by my college chaplain. He cared about me as a grieving individual, rather than about my parents or my dead sister … whereas it did feel like friends and family were much more concerned about my parents than about me.'

What makes things worse?

Again, with hindsight, the following are commonly reported as making things harder for the grieving sibling:

- being sent away at the time of the death
- being excluded from the funeral
- being left out of decisions
- other children saying hurtful things
- not being able to concentrate at school or college
- telling other people who don't know what to say.

Mourning rituals

Some features particular to the death of a child affect the bereavement and mourning rituals. These may be practical differences related to the age of the child, cultural differences related to the status of the child or differences of emphasis to do with the special relationship between parent and child.

Given the enduring nature of parental grief, strongly marked by feelings of failure and guilt, it is very important to parents that they 'do their best' for their child after death, which is one aspect of bereavement rituals. For themselves, and for others too, rituals also help to make the loss real and aid the mourning task of learning to live without the presence of the loved one. A third function of rituals is to provide social recognition of the death and public expression of the emotions aroused.

At the time of death

Most religious faiths have rites that are performed with the aid of a priest, minister or holy person, to prepare the dying for the life to come and to lay the dead to rest. Common to those of all faiths, and those with none, is the need to say goodbye to the child, which is in itself a ritual. Seeing, touching, holding and talking to the child all have added significance when the death was unexpected and sudden, and in the case of perinatal death involves saying hello as well as goodbye.

Not all believers in a particular religion keep the same observance of traditional rituals, although it is important to be aware of orthodox practice. For example, distress may be caused to both the Muslim and Hindu family if a child's body is touched after death by a non-believer, although disposable gloves may be used if the family are unable to prepare the body themselves. Removing a lock of hair would be offensive to Muslims, and strict adherents of Islam may discipline themselves to show no emotion at the death of their child, believing it to be the will of Allah. For an orthodox Jewish child, the first acts of shutting the eyes, binding up the jaw and laying the arms straight are traditionally done by a family member. Good practice in hospitals includes known protocols about what to do and who to consult regarding various cultural and religious practices.

The legal ritual of registering the death, and the practical task of informing friends, family and officialdom that the child has died, are ways in which the reality of bereavement is faced and rehearsed. The absence of formal rituals such as registration is much regretted by those whose baby died before the legal age of viability. It is so important for the family to have something to show that this baby had a life.

Funeral rites

The placing of mementoes, such as a favourite toy in the coffin or on the grave is a powerful symbol of the continuing link between parent and child beyond the grave. In different forms this practice has a universal application. The following is an observation of an American Indian custom:

'Both among the Ojibway and other Indian tribes it is a very general custom to cut off a lock of hair in remembrance of their deceased children, especially those still at the breast, and wrap it up in paper and gay ribbons. Round it they lay the playthings, amulets and clothes of the little departed. These form a tolerably long and thick parcel, which is fastened up crosswise with strings, and can be carried like a doll. They give this doll a name signifying "misery" or "misfortune", and which may be translated "the doll of sorrow". This lifeless object takes the place of the deceased child. The mourning mother carries it about for a whole year ... until the spirit of the child has grown sufficiently to be able to help itself along.'

(Kohl, 1985)

Participation in the funeral rites is important to all those who are significantly affected by the death. The question of whether young children should attend the funeral is for the parents to decide and will be considered in more detail in Chapter 5. Those who do not attend can participate in other ways, for example by being involved in decision making about the form of service, choice of music and so on.

In normal circumstances, Jewish and Muslim funerals take place within 24 hours of the death, and Hindus prefer the funeral to take place as soon as possible. If delay is unavoidable, the reasons need to be carefully explained. Coroners' officers will make special arrangements if a post-mortem is required, so that the funeral is not unduly delayed.

After the funeral

Of all the major religions, Islam upholds the most exacting mourning rituals. The family stays at home for the first three days, and food is brought in by relatives. Strict mourning lasts for 40 days, after which the grave is visited on Fridays. Traditional Hindu mourning is a communal affair, with constant visiting of extended family and neighbours. During the first 12 days after the funeral, ritualistic mourning takes place in the family home, led by an experienced female relative, to encourage the open expression of grief.

Having a place to visit, whether it be a grave or garden of remembrance, provides a continuing ritual for the expression of grief. The intense yearning to be physically close to the child again can be so great as to endanger fantasies of digging up the coffin. Initially, life may only be bearable if sustained by daily visits to the grave to reassure the child of continuing love and care. Later, the placing of the headstone is another formal ritual to mark the permanence of death.

Keeping the child's name and memory alive is a primary concern for parents, and at least a temporary concern for others too. Memorial ceremonies provide an opportunity for the child's school to celebrate the child's life and mourn his loss. Family, school and the local community may choose a form of commemoration, such as an award or dedication, or may embark on fundraising activities to benefit an organisation or area of research associated with the child.

Photographs and other mementoes may be avoided initially but eventually treasured. Sorting through the child's possessions is a painful business and may be long delayed. The distribution of mementoes in the form of toys and clothes amongst family and friends is usually much appreciated, as these are transitional objects linking the past to the future. Sadly, in the case of sudden death, there may be a superstitious reluctance for friends to accept anything belonging to the child.

Clearing the child's room is another important milestone and not one to be hurried. The choice of when it feels right to do this is an individual one and should be left entirely to the immediate family.

Anniversaries and significant times present opportunities to take stock of the journey through grief and to remember the child in a special way. Continuing rituals of birthday cards and birthday cakes are perfectly natural ways of marking 'would-have-been' milestones, and the buying of Christmas presents may be an important way of including the dead child within the living family at a special time. Those who question such a practice as ghoulish or unrealistic need only ask, does it help, or does it hinder, this parent or family?

Inscriptions in a Book of Remembrance are particularly valued by those who have few tangible reminders. Similarly, a joint memorial service, such as the Candle Service held annually in many of our major cities, when a candle is lit for every named child, is another way of using ritual to celebrate life as well as to mourn death.

References

Bowlby J (1969–80) *Attachment and Loss*, Vols 1–3: *Attachment*, Vol 1 (1969); *Separation: anxiety and anger*, Vol 2 (1973); *Loss: sadness and depression*, Vol 3 (1980). Basic Books, New York.

Freud S (1961 – originally published 1917) Mourning and melancholia. In: J Strachey (ed and trans) *The Standard Edition of the Complete Psychological Works of Sigmund Freud*, Vol 14, pp 243–58. Hogarth Press, London.

Klass D, Silverman P and Nickman S (eds) (1996) *Continuing Bonds: new understandings of grief*. Taylor & Francis, London.

Kohl J (1985) *Kitchi-Gami*. Minnesota Historical Society Press, St Paul.

Nixon J and Pearn J (1977) Emotional sequelae of parents and sibs following the drowning or near drowning of a child. *Australian and New Zealand Journal of Psychiatry*. **11**: 265–8.

Parkes CM (1972) *Bereavement: studies of grief in adult life*. International Universities Press/Pelican, New York.

Parkes CM and Brown RJ (1972) Health after bereavement: a controlled study of young Boston widows and widowers. *Psychosomatic Medicine*. **34**(5): 449–61.

Parkinson F (1993) *Post-Trauma Stress*. Sheldon Press, London.

Peppers LG and Knapp RJ (1980) *Motherhood and Mourning*. Praeger, New York.

Stroebe M, Gergen MM, Gergen KJ and Stroebe W (1992) Broken hearts or broken bonds. *American Psychologist*. **47**(10): 1205–12.

Stroebe M, Stroebe W and Hansson R (eds) (1993) *Handbook of Bereavement: theory, research and intervention*. Cambridge University Press, Cambridge.

Worden WJ (1991) *Grief Counselling and Grief Therapy* (2e). Routledge, London.

Section 2

Good practice guidelines

3 Professional roles

'Grief wounds more deeply in solitude; tears are less bitter
when mingled with others' tears.'

Seneca's *Agamemnon*

Attention is now focused on the roles and functions of various groups according to job title. Some, like the paediatric intensive care nurse or funeral director, have an essential role to play and will encounter the death of a child as part and parcel of their work. Others, such as the registrar of births, marriages and deaths, will have a single and functional contact with many bereaved families, while health visitors and social workers are likely to be involved in ongoing support. GPs and clergy may fill a key supportive role, although only occasionally over a lifetime career. Ambulance and police personnel are in the front line in emergency situations, and their initial reactions can do much to help or hinder parents. Teachers seldom deal with the death of a child, but they too can perform significant functions and be profoundly affected.

Whatever the level of involvement, this chapter will give information, reassurance and confidence. Points of likely involvement with the terminally ill child or bereaved family will be identified and linked to the possible tasks to be undertaken. Examples of good practice will be illustrated by drawing on the experience of families and individual professionals.

Different professions are considered alphabetically. If this chapter is being used for reference, the reader's attention is drawn to the general principles, which apply to everyone, in Chapter 4.

Ambulance personnel

Involvement

Ambulance personnel are often the first emergency responders on the scene, minutes after the fatal accident, onset of acute illness or discovery of the dead child. The way they carry out their duties can make a significant contribution to how the family copes subsequently. Ambulance crews are trained in resuscitation and paramedics are qualified to administer drugs. One ambulance technician in London had dealt with 10 child deaths in five years: another could recall four in 18 years. The typical pattern of response is a 999 call through the radio control system, administering resuscitation or treatment at the scene as appropriate and transporting the child to the hospital accident and emergency department, or directly to the mortuary if the death has been certified at home.

Function

The arrival of the ambulance is seen as a source of hope, and the ambulance officer as a saviour. When there is indeed hope of the child's life being saved, the obvious priority is emergency treatment and hospitalisation. When the child is already dead, however, it is usually the ambulance officer who is the first professional to confirm the fact. It is necessary for the parents to hear this unambiguous statement if they are to begin to take in the reality of what has happened. The priority is now the care and comfort of the parents and family.

In the case of sudden death at home, the ambulance crew will have a vital role to play in co-ordinating initial support. This may involve contacting the other parent, relatives, GP, clergy and explaining why the police must attend. As the first on the scene after a cot death, their reassurance to parents that the death was not preventable is invaluable.

Concerns

As ambulance personnel are trained for action, it is hard to deal with the feelings of uselessness when the child has died at home. They are faced with extreme family reactions, which are unpredictable. Later, they have their own reactions to deal with, including 'there but for the grace of God goes one of mine'. If they seek help to come to terms with their own feelings over and above the informal support available from colleagues, they risk being seen as weak and in-adequate. Perhaps the greatest fear is being called to a home death that involves suspected child abuse. This situation calls for great restraint to cope with the anger that arises when the basic instinct of saving life has been betrayed.

Good practice

The following pointers have been drawn from the experience of a county training officer in the ambulance service and a reference manual published by the Irish Sudden Infant Death Association:

'Sensitivity, common sense and good communication skills are valuable for the initial support of parents immediately after the death. These are shown by:

- treating the child with respect and referring to him by name
- offering practical help and comfort to the family
- being generous with time and not hurrying a dead child away
- explaining the bodily changes which may occur during or after the dying process, such as discoloration
- explaining what will happen and where, reassuring parents that they can see and hold the child again at hospital
- always taking mother or nearest relative with the child in the ambulance and encouraging her to hold the child.

Support for personnel affected by distress and trauma is part of building up good working practices and relationships with fellow officers and other colleagues in the health service.'

Clergy

Involvement

Many families that give little or no active support to their church will fall back on the traditional beliefs and rituals of their culture. Thus the leader of the local religious community, whether priest, minister, imam or rabbi, is nearly always involved at the time of the death or soon after. Hospital chaplains are often involved before the death of a terminally ill child, building up supportive relationships with both families and staff. In many hospitals the chaplain is on call to attend to parents of a child who has been brought into casualty or intensive care, as part of a co-ordinated team response. In maternity hospitals, the chaplain is closely involved, and will usually conduct the funeral.

Most clergy offer their pastoral support by visiting the family as soon as they hear of the death of a child in their area, often from the undertaker, and continue to visit for as long as the family wish. The priest or minister who has an accumulated knowledge of the family history is ideally placed to receive the expression of grief.

However, now that fewer than one in four babies is baptised into the Church of England, the reality is that the spiritual meaning of the church is no longer relevant to the majority.

Function

The hospital chaplain is an important source of emotional support for many parents, some of whom will derive comfort from having their young infant baptised or receiving a blessing.

Unless the family already has an allegiance to a particular church, the parochial role is restricted to conducting the funeral service. John, an Anglican priest in a town parish, describes himself as a 'necessary functionary' for death rituals in a secular society. He makes a point of visiting the family as soon as possible, 'just to listen and act as a buffer for the injustice and anger they feel'. He has learned that there is nothing he can say in answer to the question. 'Why has God done this to my innocent child?' except to acknowledge the distress. Later, perhaps, is the time for engaging with the family in a spiritual search for meaning, but for now he resists the platitudes of false comfort. Practically speaking, he can advise the family of their options and funeral arrangements, and help them to make informed choices. Parish clergy are in a good position to slow down well-meaning relatives who rush parents into hasty decisions.

Concerns

As the traditional role of the church becomes eroded, there are increasing dilemmas posed by the trend towards essentially humanist funerals. Family requests for the inclusion of popular music and secular readings may be seen as undermining the religious significance of the funeral service. Clergy are as subject to stress as anyone in the face of tragedy and may feel more exposed than most to the extent of human suffering. 'I try not to get over-involved', one priest said, 'but the pathos of some cases just gets to me ...'. Not all clergy are supported by an understanding spouse or fellow priest.

Confidentiality is an important issue, particularly for hospital chaplains, and may add to the stresses.

Good practice

David and Glenda were plunged into a nightmare when their three-year-old daughter, Stacey, suffered unsuspected heart problems during a minor nose operation and died after some hours in intensive care. The Catholic chaplain who was called to give a last blessing to

Stacey stayed to comfort the shocked and angry parents and later took them home in his car. Glenda recalls:

'He was really good with Dave, who kept on at him about God letting Stacey die. He seemed to understand, and said we had every right to be angry.'

Clergy who are experienced in this area of grief say that expressions of sympathy need to be carefully chosen. Talking of 'God's will' or 'an angel in heaven' is not helpful. Parents of babies who have not been baptised need reassurance that Christian theology no longer sees this as an exclusion from God's grace. Similarly, parents who blame themselves need reassurance that their child's death is not a punishment.

Counsellors (see also Chapter 7, pp 158–66)

Involvement

Counselling may be sought as a direct consequence of the bereavement, probably within the first year; or the loss of a child may be part of a broader picture when someone presents for counselling at a later stage with other issues, such as marital difficulties or depression. The setting for the counselling may be as a private practitioner; as a health practice or EAP (Employee Assistance Programme) counsellor; within hospital, hospice or bereavement services; as part of pastoral care; or belonging to a specialist area relevant to the death, such as termination, cancer or genetics. Counselling may have been offered to the family during the child's illness, which may enable the bereaved to work through their feelings of loss after the death. Whether self-presenting or referred, the bereaved person enters a contract with the counsellor which sets out the terms, frequency and objectives of the counselling. This is particularly important for professionals trained as counsellors who are also known in other roles – as a nurse, social worker or GP – so that the client is clear about which role they are using for the purpose of meeting. Professionals who use counselling skills within their work but who are not trained as counsellors should not, of course, lay claim to the title of counsellor, nor encourage others to regard them as a counsellor.

Function

The counsellor's main function is to provide independent psychological support. Lendrum and Syme in the introduction to *Gift of Tears* (1992) refer to being 'enabled, through the presence of another person, to work through our separate griefs and to lay down some of the burdens we had been carrying.'

Whatever the setting, the counsellor seeks to develop a therapeutic relationship within clear boundaries which will promote trust, safety, space, permission, normalisation, support and challenge. Whatever methods are used, the goal will be to find some way of integrating a sense of self before, during and after the death of the child. The relationship with the counsellor is likely to provide the opportunity to re-work issues of attachment, separation and loss.

For those who are already self-aware, the counsellor's role will be more as companion than guide. Others who are less articulate emotionally may require a more educative role from their counsellor to develop inner resources and perhaps learn new strategies.

Concerns

Typically, these are about the counsellor's ability to cope with raw and chronic grief, and the sense of helplessness which often accompanies bereavement counselling. The death of a child is specially poignant and leaves the counsellor vulnerable to her own real or feared losses, particularly in relation to her own children. For a full-time counsellor dealing exclusively with bereavement there is a concern that her normality becomes centred on death and grief in a world full of accidents and illness. A counsellor constantly exposed to child death may fear losing the capacity to respect the uniqueness of the client's experience. The following observation is made by a counsellor who is also a bereaved parent herself:

'I have heard other counsellors express the view that there is a time limit or "shelf-life" for bereavement counsellors. One counsellor actually admitted to me that she felt it was time to leave her current job because she felt that she had heard so much grief that nothing was unique to *her* any more, and she felt that she was doing her clients a disservice. A pretty brave decision when paid counselling jobs aren't easily obtainable and your salary may be important to your family.'

Good practice

Counsellors need good assessment skills, to take into account how the external circumstances of the bereavement and the internal make-up of the prospective client affect the appropriateness of counselling. The counsellor should take into account her level of training and experience in assessing whether she can meet the client's needs, and if she feels unable to do so, will offer best support by referring on. Supervision can be invaluable for these assessment issues. Adequate supervision is essential at all stages, with access to one's own therapy when needed. (*See* Chapter 4 for more on supervision.)

The counselling contract is a mutual agreement between counsellor and client about the nature and purpose of their work together. Clear contracting, clarity of task and regular reviews are all important to maintain safety, confidence and focus. Particular care needs to be given to endings – uncertain or unplanned endings may compound the client's grief, whereas well-managed endings can help the client to re-work some aspects of the bereavement. Membership of a professional association with a code of ethics and complaints procedure is necessary for safe practice and this information should be made available to the client. There is also an obligation on the counsellor to maintain professional development through reading and ongoing training.

Funeral directors

Involvement

Although legally there is nothing to stop parents managing the child's funeral themselves, nearly all will engage a funeral director to do this. Contact is usually made within hours of the death. Those firms which offer a free basic service in the event of a child's death tend to take a special pride in this very sensitive part of their work.

Function

In the first interview with the parents, the funeral director or receptionist gives information about options and requires answers to difficult questions. Is a burial or cremation preferred? When is the funeral to be? Where will the child's body lie meanwhile? While always respecting the parents' wishes, the undertaker may offer points of view the parents had not considered: in determining burial or cremation, what happens if they move house in a few years? Many parents do not know what they can and cannot do, and may need encouragement to help to dress the child, to take the child out of the coffin or to have the child at home for a while.

In preparing the body for the coffin, special care is taken to present the baby or child in the most natural and attractive way. Photos, handprints and a piece of hair are usually offered to parents.

Male relatives often wish to carry the coffin themselves, which seems more appropriate when the child is young and the coffin small. If preferred, the funeral director and staff will take responsibility for this and other practical tasks, thus freeing the family to give way to their grief.

Concerns

Keeping the balance between compassion and professional detachment can be difficult. Nothing affects staff so much as the preparation of a young child for the coffin, and they will take enormous trouble to do their best for the family. The first interview with shocked and distraught parents can be very stressful.

Good practice

A funeral director with many years' experience believes the guiding principle should be to involve the family in the funeral preparations as much as possible:

> 'I always try to take my instructions from the parents themselves, and encourage them to see and hold the child as often as they wish. If parents are reluctant to take their baby out of the coffin, I hold the baby myself first, to give them confidence and to show my respect.'

Parents should not be rushed into making hasty decisions about funeral arrangements, and value advice about different options, ranging from a full church service to a simple ceremony in the home. The option of opening a new family grave is an important consideration for parents who eventually wish to be laid to rest in the same place as their child.

General practitioners

Involvement

Typically a doctor in general practice will deal with a child death every few years, usually in the traumatic circumstances of a sudden death by accident, and occasionally as the result of chronic illness.

In the latter case, the doctor will have been closely involved with the family over a period of time and perhaps since the child's birth. He may have played a significant part in the family's experience of the diagnosis, treatment and palliative care, particularly if the death occurs at home. In the process he may have formed close relationships with the parents and child. The GP leads a primary care team who may be involved over many years with a family for whom the death of a child has far-reaching implications.

A GP looks back over many years' experience in the same three-person practice with these comments:

'With hindsight, it is clear that in the management of the bereaved family, the GP, district nurse, practice nurse, health visitor and counsellor amongst others, all play an important part in helping families through their grieving. The surprising thing to me is how long the process lasts, and the extent to which there can be ramifications throughout the family of the deceased.'

Function

The GP is a primary care provider, a central reference point of all community healthcare, and, as such, has a co-ordinating role. Assessment, treatment and referral are key functions. The GP will be a point of first contact for women who miscarry or seek termination of pregnancy. The GP's help is often sought in going through medical reports following a perinatal death. At the time of bereavement, the GP may be called on to alleviate post-trauma distress, and parents certainly appreciate a home visit at this time, particularly following a cot death. The GP provides medical information and advice. In the early days a mild sedative may be prescribed to help with sleep disturbance. Later, treatment of chronic stress and depression will range from advice to psychiatric referral, but in most cases will include some counselling and/or drugs, depending on the GP's resources and approach to mental health. Measures of healthy grieving are the frequency of visits to the practice centre, the nature of presenting symptoms, and the ability to return to work. As GPs are required to confirm fitness to work, they are in an excellent position to monitor the situation. They also provide continuity for the family and are readily accessible when other supports have fallen away. Record-keeping is an important function for providing this continuity of care, enabling the GP to relate behaviour or symptoms to previous losses.

Now that the majority of primary care practices have counselling services, it may become routine for the GP to refer any mental health concerns connected with bereavement to the counsellor, or CPN. This can result in pathologising all grief reactions and inappropriate referrals. GPs may find the comments of this GP counsellor of interest:

'It's surprising how many GPs feel uncomfortable with bereavement and often refer clients to me within the first weeks of a death, when all they really need to do is to "normalise" grief reactions. My experience has been that the message conveyed is that counselling is a compulsory part of bereavement, when in fact many people, once they realise that their feelings are normal, cope very well on their own.

The impact on siblings is often unrecognised in that I have heard a teenager being told "be strong for your mum and dad" and another "you've got your whole life ahead of you, stop being silly".'

Concerns

Lack of formal preparation and infrequent incidence of child death mean that the GP will have to call on inner resources. Traditional attitudes in the medical profession make it hard to deal with feelings of helplessness and inadequacy when a child dies. It goes against the grain for some doctors to be as open as parents would like, and many are more comfortable with sharing clinical detail than giving emotional support. Similarly, the traditional independence of doctors makes it hard to seek professional support and advice for themselves. Medical training and hospital work encourage the attitude that a doctor can cope with anything; in general practice a doctor is indeed expected to cope with everything, frequently switching from mundane to emotionally demanding tasks. On a practical level, GPs who are motivated to offer direct support have to guard their time and commitment priorities, both in the surgery and in terms of home visiting.

GPs may be subject to irrational criticism from parents. For example, it is a general pattern that parents change to another doctor after a cot death.

Good practice

In responding to a sudden death for the first time, the GP may welcome the following pointers as being valued by families.

- Showing that you care and sharing your feeling is much appreciated by parents.
- When presented with a dead child clearly beyond resuscitation, remember the value of parents being with their child *for as long as they wish* before handing over to the coroner.
- Families will welcome your reassurance that grieving is a gradual process that cannot be hurried, and that you and your team are available for ongoing support.
- In prescribing drugs to alleviate distress, be aware that many parents later regret taking any medication which impedes decision making or dulls emotions to an extreme degree.
- Advise parents of likely reactions, both physical and emotional, and reassure them of the normality of such symptoms as aching arms, distressing dreams, hearing the child's voice, loss of appetite and libido, anger and guilt.

- Encourage siblings to be involved by informing parents of the possible benefits of brothers and sisters seeing the dead child and attending the funeral.
- Explain practicalities, like the coroner's role, registering the death, funeral options.

(*See also* Chapter 5.)

Finally, these are the comments of a senior partner in a busy inner-city general practice:

'We all set ourselves high standards, so we may see a child's death as a personal failure. It is important to acknowledge and deal with these feelings. Our professional defences shouldn't get in the way of letting parents see our anxiety, uncertainty or sadness. Also, as a male GP, I can gently challenge the stereotypical father's need to "be strong". Overall, the most important thing is to be there for the family, not necessarily to do something. *Parents require human contact more than cold professionalism.*'

Community Health Council recommendations

In 1999 the Community Health Council in Cheshire commissioned a survey on *Care for the Very Ill* conducted by a Healthwatch panel of 500 local people aged over 15, as part of current NHS strategy promoting consultation with patients and public. While the survey is not specifically to do with children, some of the panel's recommendations certainly apply to older children, and they make interesting reading:

- patients should be asked how much they wish to be told about their illness following diagnosis
- opportunity should be given for further questions or provision of information at all subsequent contacts

- patients' wishes with regard to information given to relatives should be sought and adhered to
- training for professionals dealing with bereavement should emphasise a flexibility of approach, acknowledging the very different needs of individual patients
- patients should be involved, when they wish, in deciding on methods and levels of pain relief
- provision of hospice care should be supported by health authorities
- provision of independent counselling for terminally ill patients and their carers should be supported by health authorities and social services.

Health visitors

Involvement

Where long-term illness or disability leads to death, the health visitor will already be involved with the family, perhaps liaising with other agencies to provide nursery places for siblings, with benefit officers and with support organisations. She has a pivotal role in the communication protocol that follows childhood death. More districts and trusts are now publishing written procedures to formalise existing systems in which the health visitor is responsible for disseminating information from the hospital to the school, community health services and hospital staff. The health visitor has access to medical records and information about the family, knowledge of the community and local resources.

Involvement is immediate as well as automatic, and contact is made with the family as soon as the health visitor is informed of the death, possibly the same day. If the family is known, it may be appropriate to attend the funeral. Follow-up visits may continue up to the first anniversary, depending on the wishes of the parents.

Function

Immediate support on a practical level may include co-ordinating services, explaining procedures, liaising with the GP and providing medical information. Although health visitors are trained to give advice and help, in this situation they are also required to be active listeners, allowing the family to talk through their feelings. Their unique position in the community can provide excellent opportunities for addressing the needs of siblings, grandparents and the concerns of other families following a sudden death.

Follow-up after hospital visits is offered to parents, to go over the medical issues. Advice may be sought about surviving siblings and subsequent children. Mothers who are isolated may need a lot of emotional support, facing the health visitor with the dilemma of whether preventive mental health work is consistent with the role and caseload. The level of continuing support will depend partly on the individual's confidence in counselling skills and access to supervision. Referrals to other agencies for further help may be considered appropriate.

Concerns

In areas where there is no established protocol for health visitor liaison, there is always the anxiety about a loophole in communication. The resulting distress to parents when, say, a routine appointment arrives for the dead child, is deeply embarrassing. In the case of sudden death from SIDS or acute illness, the health visitor may be left with doubts and self blame: was there some sign or symptom that was missed, and were visits frequent enough?

Apprehension at the emotional turmoil of the bereaved family and how one will be affected personally is stressful. In visiting the home alone, the health visitor can take on some of the family's feelings of isolation and may well bear the brunt of parental feelings of guilt and blame, and be faced with very difficult questions with no easy answers.

There may be no support structure or formal supervision to help deal with personal reactions and assess appropriate levels of involvement. Where a need for further help for the family is identified, there may be a lack of local counselling and befriending resources.

Good practice

Detailed guidelines are to be found in leaflets published by the Foundation for the Study of Infant Death and the Scottish Cot Death Trust. The following advice is taken from discussions with several experienced professionals from different areas.

- Be sensitive to the parents' needs and go at their pace, being supportive without taking over.
- Avoid saying anything that implies judgement or criticism of the child's care.
- Be prepared to listen; share feelings and memories.
- Be there for *all* the family, including siblings and grandparents.
- Do not give up visiting for fear of intruding (unless requested to do so): continue telephone contact and remember anniversaries.
- Familiarise yourself with procedures in your area regarding hospitals, police, funeral arrangements, social services; and research local and national bereavement resources.

A health visitor provides this recent example of how her clinic supported the young mother of a four-month-old cot death baby:

'As a single parent with three other young children, Gwen needed a lot of support. My colleague was frustrated that Gwen was unwilling to do all the things advised for healthy grieving, like visiting the baby in the hospital, dressing him, having a photograph and so on. We talked it through as a team, and suggested to my colleague that there might be other members of the family who could be involved, and in fact two of Gwen's sisters were keen to help dress the baby and sort out the funeral and that's what happened. It was important for the family to be in charge.'

Hospital doctors

Involvement

Doctors may be involved in the casualty department, both at children's hospitals and at general hospitals, where they see the victims of accidents, of self-inflicted injuries and of emergency situations. Another obvious area is the intensive care unit, where, by definition, the illness is critical. Deaths occur more rarely on other hospital wards, such as from terminal pneumonia in a child with a chronic disability, or as the outcome of malignant disease and other life-threatening conditions. Here the consultant will already be a familiar and important person to the child and family, and may have been involved from the time of diagnosis, when grieving begins for many parents. Bereavement issues are also relevant to doctors involved with neonates, stillbirths and terminations for fetal abnormalities.

Function

As well as being responsible for the medical treatment of disease, doctors are concerned with the overall care of the patient, and for paediatricians the patient equals child *and* family. In the case of terminal illness, the consultant has the task of communicating the diagnosis, of explaining the progression of the condition, and keeping parents informed so that joint decisions can be made about treatment choices. This may include the crucial choice between active treatment and palliative care.

The doctor confirms the death, and if the parents are not present at the time, is likely to be the one to inform them. If the death is sudden, another task is to explain the legal process and possibility of a post-mortem. Explanations are required regarding the circumstances that have caused the death, and at this time parents need to know that they will have the opportunity of subsequent meetings to discuss post-mortem reports, answer questions relating to siblings, future children, genetic implications and future support resources. Some doctors offer routine home or hospital visits for such meetings. Hospital doctors may be interested in these comments made by an experienced GP:

> 'Anecdotally, both from my patients and from other sources, I still hear of cases where the announcement of death or impending death is handled badly. This is rather sad since I feel as a profession we should be managing the situation better. I think in hospital the junior members of the team should have an opportunity to be present at these contacts with relatives, but the sole responsibility for conveying sympathy to the bereaved and supplying them with additional information should come from the top of the team, and this should be standard practice. It is an insult to relatives and an assault on the emotional integrity of junior hospital doctors to expect them to handle that sort of situation on their own, with no previous experience and little training in this area.'

At the time of death, the doctor needs to ensure that immediate support for the family is available from the social services department, chaplain or other designated staff. In the case of the death of a young infant, other practicalities include the control of pain and lactation and help with sleep.

In all deaths, there is a communication role, to liaise with the GP, health visitor and, in certain circumstances, with the community medicine specialist.

Concerns

Newly qualified doctors may find it hard to deal with young parents and older children because of their similarity in age.

Medical ethics are involved in some issues, such as:

- whether and when resuscitation efforts should cease
- whether active treatment should give way to palliative care
- when life-support systems should be withdrawn
- the use of donor organs.

Resources can become an overriding concern. Consultants who wish to improve facilities for the child's family, or introduce policies that allow greater parental involvement, will find themselves arguing against colleagues who see death as a non-medical issue.

Professionalism and personal feelings may be in conflict, causing anxiety about one's ability to handle the situation appropriately. Should feelings be shown, uncertainties admitted? How does one develop the skills and sensitivity needed to talk to bereaved parents? And where does the healer go for healing and support?

Good practice

Parents commonly identify several points relating specifically to hospital doctors.

- Even if the consultant was not present at the death, parents appreciated the consultant visiting them to acknowledge the death.
- Knowing and using the child's name, and looking the parents straight in the eye, conveyed respect.
- Expressing regret and appropriate use of touch conveyed real caring.

(*See also* Chapter 5.)

John Sills, a consultant paediatrician at Alder Hey Hospital, Liverpool, offers this advice to junior doctors working in casualty or intensive care:

'Basically they should show that they care about what has happened, that they respect the child and the family, and that they are there to answer questions. If the death is relatively non-acute they should keep the parents informed, and should liaise with their senior colleagues about what is happening.'

Richard Wilson, consultant paediatrician at Kingston Hospital, is widely respected for his work with bereaved families. These are his comments:

'We cannot make the situation better, but we may make it worse, and we must learn to avoid doing so. But we do care and are moved by events. As professionals we want to help, yet difficulties arise in distinguishing between our emotions and needs and those of the parents. We must acknowledge our personal feelings but not let them overwhelm our professional role. The family has need of our help, but we give it not as experts but almost as passers-by whom they have allowed in. There must be organisation and guidelines, but we should have some understanding of ourselves, for only then can we be of use.

When we meet bereaved parents it is important to recognise the individuality of each situation, to know a little theory, to have tips – which come essentially from parents – on what can and cannot be done, to decide our own role, and in particular develop our ability to listen.'

Nurses

Involvement

All the areas quoted above for hospital doctors will also apply to hospital nurses. The primary nurse, a named nurse on the ward with whom parents can identify, will have a very close involvement with child and family. In the case of death after chronic illness, nurses are likely to have built up intimate relationships over many years. Neonatal nurses naturally become very attached to the babies in their care.

As a member of a primary healthcare team in the community, the nurse will be known to the family of a child who is terminally ill with cancer or a congenital abnormality.

Function

The nurse in casualty will form part of the emergency care team and, when the child dies, will have specific tasks relating to the laying out of the body. A senior nurse takes on responsibility for looking after the parents. Intensive care nurses are similarly required to carry out different roles, of technician before the death and comforter afterwards. Palliative care nurses work to ensure the control of pain and to see the child is comfortable.

Overall, the nurse administers and monitors the care plan and has a pivotal role regarding communication between parents and consultants. Whether the child dies at home or hospital, the parents are always seen as the main carers, and the professional role is advising and supporting them. Hospital nurses tend to become experts in disease, while community nurses develop expertise in ongoing support.

Concerns

The need for staff support is a big issue. Road traffic accidents and cot deaths are particularly harrowing, especially when the child is unmarked and looks perfectly normal. The laying out should not be done alone. Being with bereaved parents in the rawness of their grief is very stressful and emotionally draining. In some hospitals now there is a trained staff counsellor as well as peer support.

Management issues such as staffing quotas and time allocation create extra pressures. A ward nurse cannot give two hours to be with newly bereaved parents unless this is a priority for management too.

Many nurses are concerned with what to say to a dying child and how to answer their questions, especially when parents seek to protect them from the truth. Close contact can draw the professional into family friction and squabbles.

Community paediatric nurses can feel quite isolated if there is no built-in support, particularly if a home death happens at a weekend when hospital support systems are limited.

Good practice

Discussions with nurses experienced in accident and emergency, intensive care and palliative care highlight the importance of training in interpersonal skills to deal with the emotional demands of working with loss and grief. General guidelines which emerge are:

- be yourself: this includes being prepared to show feelings
- be honest: answer questions simply and truthfully and be prepared to say 'I don't know' rather than invent answers
- listen to what parents want, and always try to see the situation from their point of view.

More practical points at the time of death include:

- allowing the family to stay with the dead child for as long as they want
- explaining that the child will get cold and change colour
- encouraging the parents to wash and dress the child

- if the child has to stay in hospital, reassure the parents they are welcome to return.

Parents also welcome the opportunity to visit the ward and talk to the nurses after the funeral.

Being informed about procedures following a death and the options available to parents is essential, and every ward should be equipped with a written protocol for staff and information leaflets for parents.

Midwives

Involvement

The status of the midwife gives her a special kind of authority and significance for parents. She may well be the first to discover or confirm the loss of a fetal heartbeat. She will be involved with late miscarriages and the delivery of a baby who has died *in utero*, and with a stillbirth of a previously well baby who suffers birth complications. Anticipated stillbirths tend to be the responsibility of senior midwives. In the event of an early cot death, the community midwife may still be visiting the mother before handing over to the health visitor.

Function

The midwife has a key role to play in the management of perinatal death and support of the parents. She works in partnership with the mother and consultant, which gives her an interpretive role, balancing medical needs with parental wishes. She prepares the mother for what will happen and keeps her informed of what is happening. After stillbirth, the midwife has a vital part to play in helping the parents to face the reality of the death. This includes the now standard procedures of taking photographs, handprints, and encouraging the parents to touch and hold the baby. It is also a listening role, giving permission to the parents to express feelings. Midwives who recognise the importance of parents seeing their malformed baby have discovered the reassurance this provides. They will find beauty in their baby somewhere, and without this opportunity will see a monster in their minds.

Fathers have traditionally been excluded from this kind of care, and may need encouragement – perhaps from a male staff member – to take advantage of the opportunities to see and handle the dead baby. Fathers who do not wish to see the baby may need help to understand the importance of this ritual for the mother.

On a practical level, the midwife is well placed to explain all the procedures to parents regarding registration, post-mortem and funeral arrangements.

Concerns

As midwifery is about being productive, the death of a baby represents total failure. The midwife will experience her own grief, guilt and anger, which means dealing with her own feelings as well as those of the parents.

The loss of a twin presents a very difficult situation. The tendency is to encourage the parents to concentrate on their joy for the live birth, but if they do not grieve for the dead one, problems arise about rejecting the surviving twin.

In hospitals without separate rooms for grieving parents, it is a dilemma whether to care for them on a ward with babies, or on a ward with no babies. Once the mother is discharged home, the caring midwife may be left anxious about continuing support.

Good practice

Much work has been done in recent years to implement the recommendations and guidelines published by the Stillbirth and Neonatal Death Society (SANDS). These emphasise the importance of giving parents information, choices and time to make their own decisions. Parents often do not know what is possible. Decisions in which parents should be involved include the following.

- Whether and when the mother should be induced when the baby has died in the womb.
- Whether and when life-support is withdrawn if the baby is born alive but known to be dying.
- Whether to see, hold, wash and dress the dead baby.
- Whether to have a post-mortem.
- Whether to take the baby home.
- How long the mother stays in hospital.

Involving fathers, and sometimes siblings or grandparents, is now the norm in most up-to-date maternity units. Millie and Derek, whose son Ben was stillborn, will always be grateful to their midwife for her patience and sensitivity:

> 'When she first asked us if we wanted to see him, we said no – we were feeling so tired and wretched. The next day she asked us again, but I was frightened what he would look like, and Derek didn't want me to get more upset. When my mum came the midwife asked if she wanted to see the baby, which she did, and then that gave us the courage to see him. She brought him in to us, and we held him and cried together and felt like a proper family.'

In the absence of a birth or death certificate, some hospitals issue their own 'certificates' to acknowledge the baby's life. Most maternity units now have a written protocol, which gives priority to parents' wishes, and many now have a separate room or suite where both parents can sleep over to spend time privately with their baby.

An experienced midwife adds a word of caution about checklists: 'They can't tell you what to say. You have to treat everyone as an individual and be sensitive to their needs.'

Police

Involvement

Child deaths involving the police are all sudden and traumatic: accidents, murders, suicides and cot deaths. They involve the police officer in unwelcome tasks, and require behaving with great tact, dignity and compassion. The inability to rescue a child from a house fire is reported to be particularly harrowing, as indeed it is for firefighters.

Function

It is the police function to report to the coroner any sudden death where the deceased has not been seen by a doctor in the previous month, or if the cause of death is uncertain. This is not generally appreciated, so the involvement of the police in the event of a cot death has to be explained carefully. The investigating officer's task is to enquire into the circumstances of the death, view the body and have the child identified prior to hospitalisation for post-mortem. The removal of bedding and clothing to help with the pathologist's report needs to be handled with sensitivity.

'Giving the death message' is a police term for delivering news that a death has occurred, and is considered harder than dealing with the victim of an accident. The unexpected police officer knocking at the door is the stereotypical dread of all parents.

Where criminal investigations are concerned, ongoing contact with the family to keep them fully informed is not always seen as a priority for the police, but is vital to the parents.

Concerns

Delivering news of a child's death causes great anxiety about what to say and the reactions of the parents. Shifting attitudes away from the 'stiff upper lip' have brought a recognition of the distress and need to debrief afterwards with a senior or welfare officer.

Being asked for details of traumatic deaths is also stressful, with uncertainty about how much to say. There is a natural wish to protect parents, especially the mother, from unpleasant facts, and an inclination to defer to another person or later time. This can leave parents frustrated and resentful.

Seeking help for stress can be seen as a sign of weakness, with concerns about confidentiality if ongoing support is required to cope with personal reactions.

Good practice

Police forces all over the country are now recognising the importance of preparing officers for these traumatic situations, with sessions of 'breaking bad news' and 'talking to parents' being included in training programmes. The experiences of bereaved parents underline the importance of the following.

- Avoid protecting parents: they need to see and to know in order to grieve.
- Answer questions as honestly as possible.
- Involve both parents and keep the family together.
- Treat the family as you would like your own to be dealt with in similar circumstances.
- Wear plain clothes in sensitive situations, such as home visits after a cot death.
- Give parents time with their child: do not hurry them.
- Always refer to the child or baby by name.

Being well-informed helps. The officer feels more confident and the family reassured if they are clear about legal requirements, post-mortem and inquest procedures. The Foundation for the Study of Infant Deaths and the Scottish Cot Death Trust publish excellent information leaflets for police officers.

Every force has a designated person who takes on a welfare role. Some forces have organised a system of peer counsellors from all levels of staff to encourage officers to talk about their feelings after involvement with traumatic incidents.

Registrars of births, marriages and deaths

Involvement

The registrar of a medium-sized town (population 150 000) can expect to deal with one or two deaths of children per month. Registration normally takes place in the district where the child died. The informants, usually the parents, can now register the death in *any* Register Office in England and Wales. A statutory declaration is signed and then forwarded to the office in the district where the death occurred. This service may involve a slight delay before the relevant certificate can be issued, but is obviously helpful to all concerned when the death occurs a long way from home. Some registrars go out to maternity hospitals to register stillbirths and neonatal deaths, and this facility is much appreciated by shocked and grieving parents.

Function

The role of the registrar is to perform the legal requirement of recording information about the death, including data for statistics, and administering the paperwork relating to the disposal of the body. In this sense the registrar is accountable to the relevant government department – the general register office. The legislation concerning who can register, and where the registration takes place, does not allow for a mobile population. As one county service manager put it: 'We are managing a sevice in the 1990s with a framework developed in the 1830s.'

Concerns

The main concern is getting the registration done while parents are in distress. Spelling out the details of the child's death and seeing them recorded in black and white for the first time can be a gruelling experience for parents, and the registrar has to guide them through the form-filling in an emotionally charged atmosphere.

Amazingly, there is at present no statutory training for registrars, and therefore no preparation for dealing with bereaved relatives. However, a national working party is looking at introducing a national certificate of competence. Meanwhile, individual registrars already define good practice as putting people before paperwork.

Good practice

As defined by a parent:

> 'We went together to register Barry's death. There were several people waiting but the receptionist showed us to a small private room till the registrar was ready to see us. He was very courteous – said he was sorry about the reason for coming, and explained what had to be done. When Susan got upset, he put his pen down and waited till we were ready to go on. He checked he'd got all the details right, then gave us two copies of the death certificate. It may seem a little thing, but it was pleasing to see such nice handwriting.'

A registrar's comments:

> 'It's important to explain clearly to parents what my task is, and then I try to ask the questions as sensitively as possible. For example, I have to ask whether the informant was present at the death. The bureaucratic version is: "Were you present at the death?" But I prefer to ask: "Were you able to be present at the death?", which takes into account their experience in a

more human way. I make a point of using the baby's or child's name as often as possible, as a mark of respect.'

Social workers

Involvement

Fieldworkers will meet child death only rarely, when the affected family is already being supported or where a child is subject to child protection procedures.

The hospital social worker will be closely involved as part of the care team in both acute and ongoing situations, and may be the one person who remains constant to the family throughout the treatment process.

Function

The hospital social worker's primary role is to support the family and to be an advocate for the parents. This support is available to all families, regardless of status, and facilitates communication between patient, parents and staff. Advocacy means representing the parents' wishes and concerns, and acting as an interpreter and mediator; it requires good counselling skills. The counselling function can continue well into the first year of bereavement and beyond, with home visits and facilitating group support.

Practical support includes providing information about benefits and entitlements during terminal illness, helping with transport and family care at the time of the death and guiding the parents through the first days of bereavement. As well as providing information about legalities, the social worker is ideally placed to help the parents make informed choices about the funeral and to consider the needs of other family members. There may be some overlap here with the midwife, health visitor or community nurse, depending on existing relationships, making good communication essential and maybe indicating a co-ordinating role with other professionals and agencies.

Concerns

Those who have opted to work in areas with a high incidence of mortality, such as casualty or intensive care, are vulnerable to accumulated stress and need well-developed support and supervision systems. Operating as a buffer between families and professionals can also be very taxing.

Child protection social workers are faced with acute dilemmas and anxieties when the life of a child is thought to be at risk. When a child dies as a result of neglect or abuse, the professional is left with feelings of anger, helplessness and guilt, and needs intense support.

Good practice

Social workers in the hospital setting have to be willing to undertake bereavement work, be aware of the effects of grief for themselves and others, and be prepared to work in a multidisciplinary way. A commitment to the rights of parents and the advocacy role underpin all good practice. One maternity unit social worker comments:

> 'I aim to work towards parents feeling that everything that could be done, was done, and that they may be left with as few regrets as possible. If they can say this, it makes their grieving easier.'

Counselling skills are basic to all social work, although the level of sensitivity needed for this emotive area indicates the benefits of further training. In order to use these skills effectively, there needs to be an acceptance within their management structure that bereavement support is part of good working practice.

Above all, the social worker is valued by parents as a good listener and as someone who can reduce their isolation. When Jo's baby

David died, the GP gave them the telephone number of the hospital social worker:

> 'This was my first glimmer of hope … and I clutched that phone number for two weeks before making contact. She just let us talk. She introduced us to a support group of bereaved parents. They too carried a big ball of black pain around – what a relief it was to meet them.'

Teachers (*see also* Chapter 8)

Involvement

The whole school community is deeply affected when a pupil dies, and teachers are indirectly involved when a pupil's sibling or young friend dies. The staff of specialist schools for children with life-threatening conditions include physiotherapists, occupational therapists and domestic personnel as well as teachers. Hospital teachers form significant relationships with children who are terminally ill.

Function

The class teacher forms an important link between school and family when a child is hospitalised, keeping the child in touch with peers and the normality of school life. When the child dies, teachers provide models for pupils in how they react. A senior teacher may well take the lead in liaising with parents, formally acknowledging the death in school, and facilitating some ceremony or ritual to express the school's mourning. Practical tasks include amending class lists and collecting anything belonging to the child.

In the case of sudden death, teachers will have more extreme reactions to deal with as shockwaves run through the school, causing anger and anxiety.

Bereaved siblings present teachers with another challenge of what to say and how to accommodate their grief. Trusted teachers may be required to act as a counsellor and confidante for the child, or even for the parents. In the rare cases when more is required, the teacher is ideally placed to monitor the reactions of the grieving child, alert the parents and enlist specialist help.

Concerns

The effects of a teenage suicide are particularly traumatic and teachers may be concerned about aroused curiosity and copy-cat attempts. In fact, any cloak of silence increases the students' anxiety. Fears of hysterical reactions may also smother open acknowledgement of any sudden death.

A death that occurs during holidays presents special problems as to how to handle the news on return to school. If a death occurs on a school trip or organised educational holiday, when teachers are *in loco parentis*, extensive debriefing and counselling will be required.

Teachers are not always informed that a pupil has lost a sibling, which makes it difficult to respond appropriately to any problematic reactions.

Good practice

Any school that exposes students to death as a natural part of life, through nature studies, biology, personal and social education programmes, will be better placed to deal openly with the unnatural death of a child. Many secondary schools now include 'death studies' on the pastoral curriculum, and devote some in-service training time to preparing teachers by looking at their own attitudes to death. Younger children may need help with the difference between death and sleep, and are able to cope better with clear, unambiguous answers to questions. Many good books are now on the market for all ages to help children make sense of their experience (*see* Appendix C).

In practical terms, the eventuality of child death should be included in the school protocol, with clear guidelines as to who does what. Acknowledging the death is always important. Teachers should keep any of the child's work for parents to collect, if they so wish.

Head teachers, or those with special responsibility for pastoral care, need to consider ways and means of communicating information about a dying child, or the death of a child, which will impact on their pupils. While confidentiality has to be respected, good liaison with parents and the school health service or community paediatrician will make it easier to confront such a sensitive situation.

A primary school teacher offers the benefit of her experience in the loss of a pupil who died from leukaemia:

> 'When he returned to school after his transplant, I tried to treat him as normally as possible. At the same time, I kept in close contact with the parents, and the children helped to organise a sponsored swim for leukaemia research. They wrote to him and visited during his last illness. When he died, the children were told in a calm and honest way. Many of us cried and I felt it important that I did not hide my grief.'

A senior secondary teacher offers this advice to colleagues:

> 'Never underestimate pupils' feelings, as siblings or friends, and don't underestimate your own influence for good. Listen to them, and try to understand beyond the words: they may ask for your help in a roundabout way. It takes courage.'

Reference

Lendrum S and Syme G (1992) *Gift of Tears*. Routledge, London.

4 Guidelines for all

'Give sorrow words; the grief that does not speak
Whispers the o'er-fraught heart, and bids it break.'

Malcolm to Macduff when he had received news of his
wife and children's murders.

Macbeth Act IV, Scene III

Sensitivity and compassion are developed rather than taught, but there are some general principles that supply the helper with more confidence, and there are skills that can be practised. The importance of support for the helper cannot be overstated, and the purpose of supervision will be discussed. Training needs are covered by the suggested contents of a training programme, including awareness raising, listening skills and some helping strategies. Finally, all readers are invited to address themselves to the resources questionnaire at the end of the chapter.

General principles

Regardless of role or situation, the most basic principle is the importance of *listening to what individual people say they want rather than presuming what they need*. After that, it is useful to bear in mind the themes that run through the experience of families quoted in this book. Families say they want: information, choices, control and permission to grieve.

Being there is more important than what you do; listening is more important than talking

There is often a pressure to know the right things to say, and a fear of saying the wrong things. We can end up feeling so anxious that we cannot listen! Be assured that simply by being in attendance or by making your visit you are doing something useful. If you are offering emotional support by listening as well, then you are doing a great deal. You are conveying the messages that the family is *not* carrying a social disease and that you are not afraid of their pain. You are still going to feel pretty helpless, but it is important to recognise that as a feature of bereavement support, and not to let the feeling of helplessness prevent your making contact. More about attending and listening skills can be found on pages 111–12.

Be clear about your involvement

First, you need to be clear about your role and what support you are offering. This should then be made clear to the bereaved person, even if your professional title appears to make it obvious. Are you there as part of your job, or out of personal concern? Are you representing an agency? Is this a one-off contact or are you offering ongoing care? Are you offering practical or emotional support? At the outset, a named introduction is a common courtesy, and it is good practice to leave behind some written confirmation of who you are and where you can be contacted.

These may well be routine procedures, but they take on added importance in bereavement when people commonly feel impotent and confused. The newly bereaved may be particularly vulnerable to people who are keen to peddle their own belief systems. Remember, too, that many bereaved parents lose faith in any justice in the world and are sensitive to further disappointment. The helper therefore needs to be scrupulous about keeping appointments, keeping time and promising only what is realistic in terms of further support.

The issue of confidentiality also needs to be considered carefully. Reassurance should be given that private information will be treated sensitively, and that any information shared is strictly in the interests of the bereaved person. Sort out with your supervisor the conditions, if any, that would compromise confidentiality.

Use the child's name

This means so much to parents, for the name keeps alive the memory of this child. It is an acknowledgement that the child really existed at a time when it is difficult for parents to separate reality from fantasy. Saying the name also means that you are interested in the child, whether or not you knew him, and that you recognise the meaning of the child's absence. It can be tempting to tiptoe round the child, in the mistaken belief that mentioning him will upset the parent. A moment's reflection is sufficient to realise that the grief for the child is ever-present, that being 'upset' is entirely appropriate and that this response arises from our own fear of painful feelings getting in the way. Asking about the child, looking at photographs and mementoes are ways of paying respect to child and parent, and help to facilitate expression of grief.

Avoid platitudes and euphemisms

Having respect for another person, regardless of age, race and social background, is one of the core conditions for a helping relationship. Respect can be shown for the other person's feelings, thoughts and beliefs, whether or not one agrees with them. Lack of respect is shown in patronising comments, discounting remarks, moralising and platitudes.

A platitude is defined as 'an empty remark made as if it were important'. To apply well-worn phrases which so easily miss the mark is insulting. Using any phrase which begins 'At least …' only serves to undermine the bereaved person's suffering. Sadly, parents hear them all too often: 'At least you have two other healthy children' or 'At least you are young enough to have another child.'

A euphemism is a device for describing something unpleasant in milder terms in an attempt to avoid the unpleasantness. Death is riddled with euphemisms such as 'We've lost him' and 'He passed away'. It has already been pointed out how mischievous such phrases can be for children, and that their persistent use may indicate continuing denial of the reality of the death. Euphemisms should not be used by carers and helpers because they can cause misunderstanding and because they avoid reality. There is no way of dressing up the harsh fact of death.

Each bereavement is unique

First, it helps to remember that each child is a unique individual. Even a premature baby will have unique characteristics. All the particular features of the child need to be mourned, and as the child is often idealised by the parents, which is not to deny the special courage of many terminally ill children, you may be able to help them grieve for the whole child, warts and all.

Second, it is important to recognise each bereaved person as an individual and to allow them the uniqueness of their own loss without constant comparisons with others' experiences or, worse still, your own. This denies the bereaved person the opportunity to be seen and accepted for herself. Out of this attention to the individual comes the ability to see more clearly the world through her eyes. Empathy is another of the core conditions which encourage trust in a helping relationship.

People come before theory. An understanding of patterns and common features is valuable: it serves to reassure you, and shared experience is comforting for the bereaved. But you can never presume to know how it is, so avoid saying, 'I know how you feel'.

It is also useful to remember that everything has to be done again by the parents and family for the first time after the child's death –

the first meal, the first visit to a supermarket, the first Christmas, the first holiday.

Seeing is believing

It is difficult to accept the reality of death, and more so if a healthy child dies suddenly. Those who grieve a personal loss need to see some evidence to connect what they understand in their heads with what they know in their hearts. Parents want to say goodbye and feel physically close in death. Parents have the right to see their dead child, however shocking or distressing that may be. They need preparation more than protection. Your patient understanding may be required in helping them consider the pros and cons, with time to make an informed choice (*see* Chapter 1, pp 10–11; Chapter 3, p 90; Chapter 5, pp 124, 126).

The same general principle applies to whether siblings should be encouraged or discouraged to see the dead child. Children are often resentful later if they were not given the choice. Very often, children are protected from knowing the full extent of the last illness and from seeing the dying child in the last hours. Even children of a very young age benefit from being included in the reality of the situation. These sensitive issues are for the parents to resolve, but they may ask for your help in thinking them through.

Fantasy is worse than reality

Knowledge is power, and having information gives one a greater sense of control in any situation. When parental responsibility is involved, the need for information is paramount. The paternalism of the medical profession is thankfully giving way to an understanding of how important it is to keep parents fully involved and consulted. As well as being ethically correct, this enables parents to work through their reactions to the death. What is not known will be imagined, and almost invariably the fantasy turns out to be worse than the reality. Younger children have the doubtful advantage of literal imagination, which can be very confusing and worrying for them if they hear only half a story and if questions are not answered honestly (*see* Chapter 6, pp 135–7).

Involve all the family

At the time of the death the mother is often protected from harsh realities, but afterwards she tends to be the focus of attention. Ask directly after the welfare of the father and other children too. If your advice and help are sought in the practical arrangements for the funeral and other rituals, remember the benefits if all the family can be involved. Parents, children and grandparents are much more likely to be able to support each other in their grief later if they have felt included in decisions about the form of service, the wording on a wreath or headstone, and what happens to the child's possessions.

There are no experts

Of course there are those who have more experience of dealing with child death and bereaved families, and those whose training equips them for special tasks. But in most situations the person best qualified to offer support is someone who is already known and trusted by the family. Bereavement work makes everyone feel inadequate and it is tempting to look around for an 'expert' who can do a better job. The only experts on this unique experience are the family. Being support- ive is much more about being there, rather than doing something. You will, however, need support and supervision for a variety of reasons.

You will need support

If you were involved with the child's care before the death or at the time of death, you will need some outlet for your own reactions. Feelings of failure and helplessness need to be expressed without fear of being judged as inadequate. Sensitive support of bereaved families is stressful and requires recognition of the demands being made of you. You may find yourself affected on several levels: by the family's grief, by memories of your own losses, by fears for the future, by anger and frustration at feeling so powerless to help. *If these feelings are not safely discharged, you either risk your own mental health or compromise your capacity for compassion.* You may be lucky enough to have instant support available amongst colleagues, but if you are working in isolation it is essential to have time built into your work schedule to offload. This may be combined with supervision from someone responsible for overseeing your work (*see* below).

The learning points from these general principles are now summarised and offered as a check against your own experience:

- show your concern by being there for the family
- listen more than you talk
- be clear about what you are offering
- be courteous and considerate
- use the child's name
- encourage the family to talk about the child
- avoid meaningless platitudes
- respect the uniqueness of the family's experience
- enable the family to make informed choices
- pay attention to brothers and sisters
- encourage the family to share decisions
- do not underestimate the value of your support
- get support for yourself.

Supervision

Supervision means different things to different people. It can be used for monitoring, assessment, evaluation and support. Many professionals have supervision of their practice as a matter of course, often with their line manager. In counselling and psychotherapy, supervision is an essential requirement to practice, with established guidelines which seek to separate supervision from line management.

The primary purpose of supervision in relation to therapeutic work with an individual or with a group concerns the well-being of the client or group members. Supervision aims to address the question: how can the needs of the client or service user be best met? At one step removed from the actual work, the supervisor aims to support the worker in achieving this end.

Why is supervision of bereavement work so important?

- Being so close to death is stressful. When the death is that of a child, and when the death is sudden, the added dimensions of tragedy and trauma make this a very difficult area of work.
- Working with death and bereavement tends to be isolating, reflecting the lonely experience of grief itself.
- Supporting someone in grief can cause a blurring of personal and professional boundaries.
- Child death may involve litigation issues.

What are the functions of supervision?

The functions of supervision generally fall into three categories:

1 *Supportive*: to provide moral, psychological and emotional support for the worker.
2 *Educative*: to facilitate learning and understanding, to develop skills and resources.
3 *Managerial*: (with a small 'm') to clarify roles, tasks and boundaries.

All three functions have clear application to bereavement support work, whether as counsellor, befriender, church visitor, health visitor, family worker; and whether working with individuals, couples, families or groups.

The *supportive* aspects are paramount. The supervisor provides a safety net for workers to identify and discharge their own feelings and reactions. These may be in relation to their personal experience of loss and bereavement; their experience of children or their own childhood; their achievements and frustrations in this area of work. Feelings of sadness, helplessness and inadequacy which are appropriate to this work can be safely explored to prevent a protective blunting of emotions at one extreme and over-identification with the bereaved person's reactions at the other extreme. The supervisor helps the worker to monitor her own well-being. Supervision provides the space where the demands of the work can be appreciated and the efforts of the worker are valued.

The *educative* aspects integrate theory with practice, by looking together at the skills and interventions used, and by considering the relationships which underpin the work. The role of the supervisor here is to help the worker identify learning and develop further insights; to guide and inform about alternative strategies and resources; and to make sense of unfolding processes. Thus the supervisee learns to work within her level of competence and to develop her competence. The ongoing evaluation of skills, experience and training needs benefits the worker as well as the client.

The *managerial* aspects relate more to the self-management of the worker than to institutional management, though agency issues are bound to impact on the work. Managerial supervision tasks include the assessment of needs and resources; the clarification of roles; the setting of objectives; time boundaries; and ethical issues such as confidentiality and client safety. Liaison with other people and referral to other agencies may need to be considered. The supervisor's role in the managerial sense is usually to monitor, advise and co-ordinate. However, on rare occasions of questionable ethics or malpractice on the part of the worker, the supervisor is responsible for giving clear direction or for taking further action to deal with the situation.

Where can you get supervision?

If bereavement support forms a significant part of your work, you should have regular, individual supervision sessions with someone who has substantial experience in this field and is familiar with the issues. Preferably that person should be someone who is not also your line manager. If it has to be your line manager, then you should have a separate agreement for meeting together for supervision purposes, which sets this work apart from other line management functions. The major argument for supervision to be provided by someone external to the agency or employment structure is that workers should be free to explore personal issues and to own feelings of inadequacy.

Whoever provides the supervision, obvious qualifications include experience of a supervisory role and training in supervision; a working knowledge of loss and bereavement issues; and an understanding of child development and family dynamics. When the supervision involves groups, a working knowledge of group dynamics needs to be added to the list.

Some of the supervisory functions listed above can be performed in a supervision group. Such a group can be made up of colleagues within the same work setting, or it can have a multidisciplinary membership of professionals or volunteers concerned with similar issues. A group of experienced people can run this as a peer group very successfully, though without an objective facilitator some of the benefits and requirements of supervision are lost. Where resources permit, the ideal situation includes both peer group supervision and individual supervision.

Training

There is a strong case to be argued for loss and bereavement issues to be included on any basic training course in the health and caring professions, so that everyone has an opportunity to prepare themselves mentally. Specialist short courses follow more naturally when some experience has been acquired.

The starting point for any training input is raising awareness of the personal anxieties that threaten to get in the way of dealing compassionately with others. The taboos associated with death in the Western world can be challenged only by confronting our fears and prejudices.

Awareness

Reflecting on our own losses enables us to:

- identify reactions and ways of coping which give insights into others' experiences
- recognise areas of loss that have been difficult to resolve
- realise that working with someone grieving a similar loss will trigger associated reactions to our past and feared losses
- acknowledge the difficulty of dealing with death in terms of our own mortality.

Acknowledging concerns that commonly beset those who support the bereaved is a reassuring exercise. Such concerns include:

- how will I cope?
- will I get sucked into others' distress?
- I won't know what to say or do
- should I show my feelings?

Acknowledgement of our own limitations helps to make these anxieties more manageable. A sense of vocation is associated with professions that seek to heal, empower, develop and support other people. It is therefore important to be prepared for the following feelings:

- feeling powerless to help

- a sense of failure and even guilt
- being inadequate for the task.

These reactions belong to the nature of grief. They do not deny the value of your support and care.

Skills

The two foundation skills required for bereavement support are basic to all effective communication: attending and listening. They are, of course, interrelated. Both sound simple but can be extremely difficult in practice, particularly when dealing with painful feelings. The learning points summarised below are best made by setting up exercises that allow participants to experience the effects of good and bad practice.

Attending

Paying attention means being alert to someone and being interested in what they have to say, which communicates the message that they are of value. That in itself encourages trust and free expression, and has a healing effect. Attending means suspending one's own concerns and prejudices, and being in a state of 'not knowing'. As well as conveying respect, attending also enables the listener to observe the whole person as communicated by body language and non-verbal behaviour. Good attention is demonstrated by:

- setting the scene: even before the communication starts, the way in which a person is greeted conveys respect
- making eye-contact is crucial; facial expressions, nods and grunts also provide physical evidence of being attended to
- removing barriers such as desks, equipment and papers, and sitting at the same level
- avoiding distracters such as bleeps and telephones.

Listening

Listening is a complex activity. It includes:

- giving attention
- receiving information
- taking in the thoughts and feelings conveyed
- interpreting behaviour
- noticing key points and themes
- checking that you have heard and understood correctly.

The focus remains on the speaker when the listener reflects back what has been heard. Restatements, paraphrasing and summarising the messages received form an important part of the process for several reasons:

- the speaker is assured of your understanding
- if you have got it wrong, the speaker can correct you
- the speaker can hear the effect of what she is saying.

Listening involves considerable self-discipline. It means suspending your own assumptions, judgements, advice and solutions. It may also mean tolerating silence, allowing the speaker time and space to gather thoughts and give expression to feelings.

Helping strategies

While active listening forms the cornerstone of bereavement support, to facilitate the expression of the disordered thoughts and feelings of grief, other approaches may be required for ongoing support. More directive strategies may also be indicated when the bereaved person finds it difficult to talk, or when uncompleted mourning tasks have been identified.

Most of the ideas that follow are simple but can be powerfully effective. A training event is the ideal opportunity to try them out on yourself and colleagues.

Prompts

Some people welcome invitations to talk about their loved one, particularly if they have been discouraged from doing so by others. Open questions about the child might be:

- 'Can you tell me more about …?'
- 'What sort of child was he?'
- 'What are your special memories?'

Photographs and mementoes provide a fund of recollections, and a genuine interest in sharing them encourages warmth and trust.

Linking

One of the tasks of mourning is making sense of what has happened, and finding a place for the loss which offers some meaning. The bereaved may need some help in linking the past to the present, and this can be done by talking them through the process of change, perhaps over three meetings.

1 Invite reminiscences of what life was like before the child died – a typical weekday, holiday and so on – for self and family.
2 Ask for a (repeat) rehearsal of the events at the time of the child's death.
3 Invite reflections on how life has changed after the child died, and how things are different now.

Rituals

Bereavement is made up of many little goodbyes, and it may be appropriate to construct together some private rituals to help the bereaved deal with difficult memories. For instance, a parent requested help with revisiting the road junction where her daughter had been killed years previously. Another parent helped her child grieve for a friend, whose funeral they had been unable to attend, by releasing helium balloons with goodbye messages on them.

Writing

For many parents and siblings, writing becomes an important therapeutic tool. When such writing can be shared, it is a powerful communicator of inner feelings.

For those who are anguished by things left unsaid to the child, the device of writing a letter, addressed as it were to the child, can be liberating. Alternatively an audio tape could be made, with messages interspersed with favourite music.

Drawing

Children are less inhibited about drawing than adults, and may derive greater benefit from pictures than words. Images and colours help to give shape to memories and complex emotions.

Scrapbooks

This is another useful approach with children, but is equally valuable to adults, and a great activity to include all the family, or the child's schoolfriends. Photographs, keepsakes, written memories, pictures of favourite pop stars and activities can all contribute to a shared album of memories. This may be a useful suggestion when one of the family is left with an impossibly idealised picture of the child, as the scrapbook can easily accommodate different images – the comic and the naughty as well as the sad and the good.

Geneogram

This is a diagrammatic way of depicting the family, like a family tree, which records births, marriages and deaths and provides a tool for exploring family relationships. It is drawn up with the help of the bereaved, and is useful for gaining a wider perspective on the significance of the child's death for different family members.

(*See also* Chapter 7, pp 163–4.)

Resources questionnaire

All readers are invited to assess their resources and needs by considering these questions.

1 How does my personal experience affect my attitude to bereavement?
2 What is the level of awareness of my own actual and feared losses?
3 Can I identify the other person's needs, and the tasks involved in my support?
4 What is my role?
5 What relevant skills do I have?
6 How do I recognise my limitations? Am I being honest, or modest?
7 Do I have training needs?
8 Do I know when, how and where to refer on for more specialist help?
9 Are my needs for consultation and support being met?

5 Guidelines for stressful situations

> 'I am not mad; I would to heaven I were!
> For then, 'tis like I should forget myself
> O, if I could, what grief should I forget!'

> Constance, on the death of her son Arthur

> *King John* Act III Scene IV

There are certain key situations when the words, actions and attitudes of professionals can have a lasting impact on the family, for good or ill. Advice may be sought by parents who are emotionally vulnerable. Others may be temporarily hostile towards those who seek to help them. Years later, parents tend to remember with utmost clarity the detail of turning points in their child's illness and treatment. And in the heightened sensitivity of their grief, thoughtless comments add to their pain just as caring gestures are treasured.

Knowing this adds to the sense of heavy responsibility at such times for professionals to 'get it right' or at least avoid 'putting one's foot in it'. Anxiety is a natural response when faced with painful emotions and a sense of helplessness. There are no blueprints for any given situation, but some general guidelines can provide signposts.

It needs to be stressed that each situation is unique and people's reactions are unpredictable. No-one can get it right all the time, but the sincerity of trying to do one's best is what matters.

Breaking bad news

One father recalls how much it meant to him that when his son died the doctor was visibly upset at the bedside. By contrast, one mother is still outraged, 10 years later, that the doctor yawned after telling her that her daughter had just died. Another mother remembers: 'We held her until the Sister said "she's gone now", and I hated her so much I could have done murder – but I know I needed to hear the words to believe it.' The task of communicating bad news is unenviable, whether at the time of diagnosis, treatment results, accident, post-mortem results or inquest. It gives rise to similar reactions as experienced when being on the receiving end: anxiety, fear, panic, anger, helplessness, failure, sadness, despair. Some of the anxiety may be about the other person's reactions, because the bearers of bad news have been known to be lynched! The message-carrier is certainly an easy target for first reactions of angry disbelief, particularly as a member of the medical profession.

A simple checklist is offered below to help identify the ideal circumstances for breaking bad news.

Why?

This may seem obvious, but the underlying question is an ethical one and raises issues of information and control. Is the amount of information given on a 'need-to-know' or 'right-to-know' basis? Nothing enrages parents more than discovering later that information about their own child has been withheld.

When?

The answer to the above will determine the timing. On a 'right-to-know' basis, the guideline must be: as soon as possible.

By whom?

Qualities are favoured more than position: ideally, it should be someone known and trusted, who shows sensitivity and has good communication skills. Most parents say it helps if the person has a continuing involvement with them, rather than someone who appears and then disappears. The importance of the authority of the person seems to depend on the nature of the information. A complex diagnosis, for example, requires specialist knowledge to answer parents' questions. In other hospital situations, the nursing staff offer more continuity.

Where?

Parents invariably recall the setting, and there is a strong association with the room and the importance of the occasion. The place should be somewhere comfortable, private and without interruption.

How?

If at all possible, the breaking of bad news should be in a face-to-face situation, and it is important to look the person in the eye. Take a few minutes before going into the situation to check your demeanour and gather your thoughts. If a telephone call is unavoidable, due consideration needs to be given to the likely impact of shock and distress.

Every effort should be made to tell both parents together. If this is not possible, another family member or friend should be present for support.

The message should be unambiguous to avoid misunderstanding, and questions should be answered as honestly as possible. Euphemisms are not helpful. In the case of giving a diagnosis of terminal illness, a balance needs to be struck between realism and hope.

Shock and disbelief may require time for the information to be received, so it is important to go at their pace. This means checking out their understanding of what you have said, and repeating or restating the information as necessary.

Check their responses: ask how they are feeling, what are their immediate concerns, are there any questions they want to ask. Some people react to bad news with denial, apparent apathy or by trivialising it, and these defences need to be respected. Before leaving the interview, ongoing support and follow-up needs to be ensured. This may involve transport arrangements, medical attention, alerting local resources and providing reassurance that there will be opportunities for addressing questions and concerns at a future time.

Finally, you will need the support of a colleague, ideally to accompany you or at least to debrief you afterwards.

Some experiences of parents

'Christine had various tests at the hospital, but we weren't told what they were for. Then one day we had a letter informing us that Christine had been diagnosed as a cystic fibrosis child and we were to visit the clinic in three weeks' time. We had no idea what cystic fibrosis was. A friend gave us the address of the Cystic Fibrosis Fund and we sent off for some leaflets.'

'We pinned all our hopes on Jason having this operation to remove the tumour. He seemed to recover very well, but the consultant was doubtful. Then Jason went downhill fast, and in the end the consultant sat down with us and said there was nothing more they could do for him. We'd got to know him quite well and it was like we were all in this together. He answered all our questions and we looked at the options. He taped that session and gave us the tape to take home: it was a great help to go over it again and play it to our parents. You can't remember half of what's said otherwise.'

'Tracy lived for 11 days. I'm usually squeamish about illness and medical things, but I wanted to know every detail about her condition. The doctor went through the post-mortem and answered all my questions as best she could – she was honest about not knowing all the answers – but it was so important for me to know all there was to know. My mum came with me, which was a help.'

'The police officer who called said that the paramedics had taken Simon to hospital and there was still hope of reviving him. It wasn't till we got to the hospital two hours later that we discovered he was dead when they found him. We felt so resentful about that lie. Did the policeman think he was doing us a favour? Our son was dead for over two hours and other people knew it and we didn't. The hospital doctor who confirmed the death was cold and detached. We wished he had shown some feeling, at least said he was sorry.'

Emergency procedures and intensive care

'We recognise that relatives have a part to play in our work, and that we help to create memories which will affect them for the rest of their lives.' So says the clinical nurse specialist at the accident and emergency department of Wythenshawe Hospital, Manchester, where the consultant and casualty team follow an enlightened policy that allows parents to be involved and fully informed throughout treatment. Lack of information and involvement are the most consistent regrets and resentments of parents of children receiving emergency medical care.

Traditionally, the care of patients' relatives has been seen as a nursing issue, as death is not a medical problem. However, more and more consultants have a growing understanding of bereavement support as part of the total healthcare package. At Alder Hey Children's Hospital in Liverpool, the prevailing philosophy is that the family is the patient, not just the child. Given this commitment, traditional objections to involving the family can be faced and overcome. More hospitals in the UK now operate open access to parents, which means they need never be separated from their child.

Protocol

The unpredictability of an emergency makes it impossible to lay down any set protocol for dealing with relatives, whose reactions are not consistent. The family's trauma is matched by the frantic efforts of the staff to save the child's life. Some parents merely wish to be reassured that something is being done, while others want to be present to see exactly what is going on. However, some general principles will guide good practice for the benefit of parents and help staff deal better with the feelings of failure when a child dies.

Teamwork

The staff team, from cleaner to consultant, will need to work through their own feelings and reactions in order to adopt a team approach. The team may also include the chaplain and social worker. Good team relationships are essential to the kind of flexibility and communication required.

Identified person

Someone on the team needs to be allocated to the care of the parents, to explain what is happening and to facilitate their needs short of obstructing treatment. Parents need to be prepared and cautioned about what they will see. When parents do not wish to be present during treatment, they will need to be kept closely informed. The identified person may be allocated by role: it may be the social worker or chaplain who routinely acts as parental support. A medically trained person may be thought more appropriate for answering questions and explaining treatment procedures.

Resuscitation

The attendance of parents during resuscitation is a contentious issue, and professional misgivings have to be challenged as well as respected. Common objections are:

- staff feel inhibited
- parents need protecting from seeing aggressive treatment
- parents get in the way
- staff are vulnerable to criticism.

These fears stem from being faced with other people's acute emotions and the defences which are erected to cope with one's own feelings. These *can* be confronted successfully once the right of parents to attend, if they wish, is accepted. In practice, staff find that parents who attend resuscitation are more concerned with the child than the treatment.

An implication is whether parents can then be involved in the decision about when resuscitation efforts should cease, always a difficult time for staff. If, when all hope has long gone, parents are unable to face the reality, the consultant has to take professional responsibility for the decision.

There are some situations where the decision to withdraw life support is fraught with difficulty. After accident-related trauma, certain criteria to establish brain stem death have to be met, which may entail necessary delay before the life support machine can be switched off. This demands particular sensitivity in explaining the situation to parents.

For most parents, being there at the moment of death and being able to touch or hold the child are essential to feeling they did all they could, that the child was not alone amongst strangers, and that they were able to let him go. All family members should have an opportunity to say these goodbyes, including young siblings, as long as this is acceptable to the parents.

Practicalities

It is necessary to have a separate room for relatives, of course, but also important to have a private space where the parents can be with their child immediately after the death for as long as they wish. Their primary support person needs to be available to them during that time without pressure from colleagues to be elsewhere. Procedures and options need to be explained, with a written booklet for reference on leaving. Parents who find it difficult to leave the child may find comfort in leaving something personal with the body. It is much appreciated when staff handle and address the child with the same warmth and respect as before death.

After the death

This is a time when professionals who are correctly informed and aware of the issues can be very helpful to bereaved families. Parents who are plunged into grief will usually need the guidance of the nurse, doctor, social worker or chaplain, particularly when the death was unexpected. Even families who can draw on the experience of other bereavements are unlikely to feel confident of their rights and obligations when a child dies. Their need for advice and guidance is never greater than at this time, not to take control away from them but so they can make their own informed choices. The assumption should not be made, as it often is, that bereaved parents – especially the mother – are not in a fit state to make decisions.

Sudden death presents the biggest challenge. There has been no preparation and there is no continuity of care. The availability of hospital social workers and chaplains will be variable. Many hospital doctors see their role finishing with the death of the child, leaving follow-up care to nursing staff or to other professionals.

Clearly the scandalous practice of organs being removed at post-mortem and retained as hospital property, without parental consent, as uncovered in 1999 at Alder Hey and other hospitals, was a betrayal of trust and a denial of human rights. Parents have been doubly bereaved and traumatised.

Roles and responsibilities need to be clear

The first and most important guideline, therefore, is to ensure adequate systems are in place, and that staff induction programmes make them known. Co-ordinated care avoids the 'rugby pass' type of management.

A designated person should be responsible for the ongoing care of parents or for co-ordinating that initial support, in line with Department of Health guidelines.

The family's GP should be informed as soon as possible as the most obvious primary care co-ordinator in the community.

Giving advice and information

Information given to parents must be accurate and consistent, with an opportunity to talk it through rather than simply being offered it in written form.

Hospital staff should be aware of cultural and religious differences, with access to translators in case of language difficulties, and to signers for the deaf.

When decisions need to be made, parents should not be hurried to suit hospital routines, and time should always be allowed for parents to change their minds.

It helps to remember that the child continues to belong to the parents, except for the coroner's brief legal 'ownership' in the case of a post-mortem. For example, talking to parents about when they are 'allowed' to see their child denies their *right* to do so.

Practical examples of the kind of information required follow.

Legalities

By law a doctor must confirm the death.

The death is then registered with the registrar for births, marriages and deaths, by either or both parents, whether married or not. In extreme circumstances, someone else present at the death or during the last illness can do this. In the case of a newly-born baby, the birth can be declared at the same time as the death is registered. The registrar issues:

- the death certificate, for which a small fee is payable
- a white BD8 form for the DSS
- a green disposal form, which is needed by the undertaker to remove the body from hospital, unless a post-mortem is required.

However, the parents are entitled to remove the body themselves once a doctor has confirmed the cause of death. This situation may arise when the child dies after 5 pm and the parents are unwilling to leave the child in the hospital mortuary overnight or over the weekend before they can register the death. Parents have the right to know that this option is available to them, however undesirable this course of action may appear.

In cases of sudden death or where the cause of death is not known

- The doctor must inform the coroner.
- The coroner's officer, usually a police officer, will visit the hospital and/or home and interview parents.
- A post-mortem examination is normally required.
- Once a medical cause of death is established, the death can be registered and the body released. In the case of a coroner's post-mortem, the coroner issues the death certificate. If no inquest is required, however, the parents are given leave to register the death.

Parents should be asked if they want to know what the post-mortem examination entails. Many do not like to ask, but are later filled with remorse for not knowing, and may suffer from fantasies of butchery. Reassurance of standard procedures and sensitive handling of the body are welcome.

In cases where a post-mortem is not legally required, it may still be requested for the sake of medical research, and is then a matter of choice. Post-mortems are forbidden to Muslims unless ordered by the coroner, and are problematic for Hindus.

Access to the child's body

It is essential that the parents are given privacy to spend as long as they wish with the child after death in hospital. It is helpful for one of the nursing staff to prepare them for the changes that will occur in the temperature and appearance of the body. They should be invited to take part in the washing and dressing of the child's body and other laying-out procedures, but should not be pressed to do so. Practising Muslim, Hindu and Jewish families are responsible for attending to the body to carry out traditional post-death rituals.

The taking of a photograph or lock of hair is now routinely offered by most hospitals, although the family's permission must be obtained: it is important to Muslims that the hair is not cut after death.

Parents are often very anxious to know where the child's body is taken after they have said their goodbyes. Again, they often do not like to ask: they are swept along in a personal nightmare and feel constrained by institutional procedures. They need to be told exactly what will happen to the child, where the body will be kept, who will tend to it and when they are able to visit. Ideally an 'open access' policy enables parents to come back to the hospital and spend time with their child at any hour of the day or night.

Options for where the child rests before the funeral

It is incumbent on professionals to make parents aware of the options, as some parents do not realise that they can have their child's body at home for some or all of the time before the funeral. Those families who have exercised this option have found it very beneficial. Again, it is a question of giving control back where it belongs.

Burial or cremation?

Parents naturally shrink from the thought of either burying or burning their child's body. Muslims are always buried, never cremated. All adult Hindus are cremated, but infants and young children may be buried. Orthodox Jews are always buried, but those of a more liberal persuasion may choose cremation. Where religious faith allows a choice, parents may welcome talking through the pros and cons with an objective outsider before making such an irrevocable decision. This means allowing time for making informed decisions. Having a specific place to visit is an important consideration for most families. An unforeseen dilemma can later occur when a grandparent or other relative generously offers to open an existing family grave so that the baby or child is not 'alone'. This may be an attractive idea at the time, but can be later regretted with the realisation that the parents are then unable to join their child after death, as they would if they had opened a new family grave. These are Lisa's reflections:

'I was in such a daze after Carl died, but I knew I didn't want him buried. I couldn't have coped with the thought of his little body under the ground. There's a special garden of remembrance in our town where the ashes of babies can be scattered, so that's what we did. It seemed a nice idea to have him with other children. But I wish someone had told us that we could have bought a special little plot there. When we visit, I envy other parents who can plant flowers and have a little plaque to sit by.

Another thing I realised too late, after talking to other mums, was that I could have had Carl home before the funeral. They were very good at the hospital and let us visit him, and then we went to see him at the chapel of rest, but it was never long enough. I'd have liked him home for at least a couple of days.'

Funeral expenses

Funeral costs vary and it is advisable to obtain more than one quotation. Some funeral directors deliver a free basic service for any child who dies under the age of 16. Parents who can ill afford a funeral may reject this as charity, and need reassurance that a free service is of equal quality and is likely to indicate a particular sensitivity to child death situations. The hospital has an obligation to arrange and pay for the funeral of stillborn children, whether born in hospital or at home.

Families receiving Income Support or some other DSS benefits are entitled to help with some or all of the funeral costs, and with the cost of transporting the body within the UK if the child dies away from home. The hospital social work department will help with the application to the Social Fund (form SF200).

Attending the funeral

The funeral presents a ritual opportunity for family and community to say final goodbyes, and for others to pay their respects to the grieving family.

The advisability of young children attending funerals

Parents often consult professionals about whether their young children should go to the funeral. This is really a question of what adults can tolerate. Any temptation to tell parents what to do should be resisted. It is much more helpful to explore with them the pros and cons, to offer points of view they may not have considered, and encourage them to trust their own judgement. When parents are caught between their own instincts to take the children and the disapproving voices of older relatives, the task is one of reassurance.

Most children who were denied the opportunity to attend a sibling's funeral later regret this. Those who would not have wished to go regret not being given the choice. The age at which children can be trusted with such a choice will depend on the degree of openness in the family.

It is more of a dilemma for the professional when it is obvious that the parents have simply assumed that children should not attend funerals and have not considered the possible benefits of taking them. Should the parents' unconsidered judgement be challenged, or is this professional interference? The use of open questions is helpful here, for example:

- 'Have you thought about other options?'
- 'What has led you to make this decision?'

Professionals attending funerals

The public part of the funeral is the proper place for all affected by the death of the child to share their grief. Nurses, teachers, social workers, health visitors and doctors who have been closely involved with the child and family may wish to attend on their own behalf, or to represent their agency. Either way, it means a lot to the family to know that they were there. Rotas may limit the numbers of staff who can go, but managers who recognise the importance of key staff attending this ritual will try to accommodate their requests.

On first visiting the family

With or without previous knowledge of the family, the first visit to the home after the bereavement is fraught with anxiety. Typical concerns are:

- will the family welcome my visit?
- is it the right time to go?

- what can I say?
- will I be overwhelmed by their grief?

There is no magic formula to dispel the apprehension, but self-preparation can help to prevent unnecessary stress. Many of the following points relate to common sense and common good practice, but in the context of heightened emotions they can easily be forgotten.

Be realistic

Part of the anxiety comes from believing that you have to know the right thing to say that will help to ease their pain, so it is immediately freeing to acknowledge to yourself what an unrealistic expectation this is. Nothing you can say or do will help to bring back the life of the child, which would be the only thing to make the family 'feel better' at this time. You are guaranteed to feel helpless as a result.

Be realistic about the amount of follow-up support you can offer, so that you do not end up promising more than you can maintain.

Be prepared

It helps to double-check the information you have about the family, in particular the name and age of the child. Allow for more time than you might generally give to a home visit. If this is the first time you have been involved with the family, or when the death is sudden, it is likely that the full story needs to be told. To do justice to the child's memory and the parents' feelings, the story should not be rushed. Learning how to end your visit and when to withdraw is a skill that comes with experience! It is made easier if you say at the beginning what time is available to you. It is useful to remember that your visit will be emotionally draining for the family as well as for you. If you can, arrange your timetable so that you allow for the impact on you, by setting aside time afterwards to debrief with a colleague.

Be clear

Introduce yourself and say who you are representing. If you are not expected, check whether your visit at this time is convenient. The purpose of your visit may be obvious to you, but at a time of such confusion it is important to say what it is. In the first few days, the family may be visited by many different professionals and befrienders. It is helpful if you leave details of your name, organisation, contact number and availability. Make it clear whether you will visit again, and if so, when that will be. An unscheduled visit from the GP or clergy can leave the family with unrealistic expectations of future visits which turn to disappointment. It is a good idea to follow up your first contact with a telephone call or a note if no other arrangement was made on your departure.

Be honest and genuine

The general principles detailed in Chapter 4 are all relevant, none more so than the warning against platitudes, which have a nasty habit of slipping out at times of anxiety. Nerves can also lead to inappropriate trading of your own experience, which should be firmly resisted, especially on this first visit. Bland reassurances do not comfort. A parent recalls the words of a visiting priest: 'You must remember that God's only son suffered on the cross for us.' The parent replied: 'Yes, but he didn't suffer for 18 months, like my son.'

If you feel lost for words, it does no harm to say so. A touch of the hand can say far more than words.

Accepting periods of silence and displays of emotion may be the most difficult but most valuable gift you can offer.

Anniversaries

Anniversaries are powerful replays of events and the emotions that accompanied them. Many parents find that the anticipation of the anniversary, during the preceding days, is as bad or worse than the day itself. Significant anniversaries also include the 'might-have-been' birthdays or other celebrations, as well as turning points in the terminal illness or events leading up to the death.

A contact of some kind by carers at the time of the anniversary of the death – particularly the first – is very much valued by the family, whether or not active support is ongoing. Many bereavement support organisations recommend a minimum of 13 months' support in order to help the bereaved through the first anniversary.

The contact that is made, by card, letter, telephone or visit, should always refer to the child by name. For example, the simplest wording on a card might be: 'To Andrew's family, with kind thoughts at this special time'.

If you are in regular contact with the family, do not be afraid of talking about the anniversary beforehand. Your support may be helpful in thinking through their options for marking the occasion, or in working out strategies for simply getting through the day.

For those who fantasise about rejoining their loved ones, the anniversary of the death may focus any suicidal thoughts. If your relationship with the parents allows, it is better to confront such thoughts than avoid them – *see* below.

Suicide risk assessment

Suicidal thoughts are common to bereaved parents, particularly in the first year of bereavement, and can be anticipated as normal. Contrary to public myth, you cannot put such ideas into people's heads by mentioning them. Fears of self-harm are generally diluted by talking about them and having them acknowledged. Although it is dangerous to generalise, the following pointers may help you to assess the risk of actual self-harm.

Usually a statement or implication of suicidal intent is concerned with ending one's misery rather than one's life. Typical comments are:

- 'I want to be with him and hold him again.'
- 'I want to go to bed and not wake up again.'
- 'Life is meaningless without him.'
- 'I can't go on like this.'
- 'He needs me more than the rest of the family.'

Such a remark needs an acknowledgement that you have heard the desperate feelings conveyed. An appropriate response might be:

'You sound as if you don't want to go on living – is that so?'

If the reply is affirmative, the next step is to ask whether that means a conscious wish to die:

'Do you mean you want to end your life?'

This feels very risky, but be assured that in nearly all cases this question will draw a conditional response, such as:

'Yes, I think about it, but I wouldn't do anything because …'

Now you can relax a little, and safely invite further exploration of how those awful feelings are experienced, and try to convey some understanding of their validity. But what if your question draws a different response:

'Yes, I've thought it all out.'
Or, simply, 'Yes.'

In this situation, the alarm bells are now ringing. Having gone so far, you need to follow with a question that will give a clear indication of purpose:

'Have you thought what you would do?'

Do not be afraid of asking this question, as it is key to the assessment of risk. The response may again be conditional:

'Well, I've thought of crashing the car, but I couldn't bear to hurt the rest of the family even more.'

Now you are dealing with some intent, balanced with reservations, which can be strengthened with your support. However, the response may be more specific:

'Oh yes. I have got the pills all saved up, and I know exactly how many to take.'

Such a detailed method needs to be taken as a serious statement of intent. This is rare, but if you are faced with this situation, *you must seek support and advice.* The ethical question of whether you should take any action without this person's consent needs to be considered. If you conclude that you should alert someone else with your worries, you must inform the person you are supporting that you are doing so out of concern for their safety and welfare.

Again, the need for good support and supervision for yourself is underlined by any doubts you may have on this score.

Further reading

Buckman R (1992) *How to Break Bad News: a guide for healthcare professionals.* Papermac, London.

6 Guidelines for talking with children

'Sorrow makes us all children again.'

Ralph Waldo Emerson

Introduction

This is an area which understandably causes a lot of anxiety. What to say, and how to say it, are the two big questions for parents and teachers facing the task of informing siblings and peers of a child who is dying, or has died. Medical personnel will also face these dilemmas, alongside the parents, with the child who is terminally ill. It goes against the grain to expose children to the harsh reality of another child's death, when the instinct is to protect them from pain. Talking to children about death also exposes adults to feelings of helplessness and uncertainty, making them vulnerable to questions which may have no answers.

What we do know is that children suffer more from ignorance than honesty, and that children are surprisingly resilient given a supportive environment.

Whilst anxieties centre on what to tell children, the first move may come from the child asking for information, usually when the adult is least prepared! Either way, the desired outcome is a dialogue between adult and child, which involves as much listening as talking. Talking *to* children becomes talking *with* children.

In situations where the child's needs indicate special attention, it is important not to make the child feel more different and isolated than she already feels as a result of her experience. Involve her family, peers, or other trusted adults as far as possible.

The guidelines offered here are based on general principles and may be applied to most situations. In extreme cases, when the child has been exposed to severe trauma, referral to a specialist should be considered.

Readers of this chapter should also refer to Chapter 2, pp 54–7, regarding the development of children's understanding of death, and to Chapter 8. Further advice for parents is offered in Chapter 7, pp 174–5.

Child experience of loss and bereavement

Although child and adult experiences of grief are different, children are people and children do grieve, even very young children. Their understanding of loss and death will obviously vary according to age and ability, so that explanations need to be age-appropriate.

Young children under five see death as temporary, and need repeated confirmation that the dead child will not be coming back. Up to age six or seven, children go through a stage of 'magical thinking' when they don't yet know the limits to the power of their own thoughts and wishes. Thus, they are particularly vulnerable to feelings of guilt and responsibility for the death, however irrational that may seem to an adult. Professor Yule, joint author of *Wise Before the Event*, says:

> 'The younger kids are, the more likely they are going to think they could have done something about it, a kind of magical thinking that they could have protected someone.'

Children between six and 10 become aware of the reality of death, gradually developing an understanding that dead means 'can't breathe, can't move, can't feel', and that death is universal and inevitable. Although they are more aware, they may not understand the feelings they are experiencing or associate them with their loss, and may become distressed as a result. Thus, a child who is not yet emotionally mature enough to talk about feelings may 'act out' her grief through aggressive behaviour or disturbed sleep.

From the age of 11 children begin to develop a more adult concept of death, and may learn to cope with the awareness of their own mortality through black humour and bravado.

An important aspect of bereavement for children is the *secondary losses* which follow from the loss of the child who has died (Hindmarch, 1995). So, for example, a child may be affected more by losing the attention of a grieving parent than by the death of a baby brother she never knew. Loss of security, trust and normality following the death of a sibling or friend may have implications reaching far beyond the immediate loss of their physical presence and companionship.

The biggest issues for children, as reported by children them-selves, sometimes long after the event, are to do with *information* and *involvement*. Children who seem to cope best are those who are kept informed about what is happening, are told about the death in unambiguous terms, and are involved in rituals such as the funeral. Children who are protected from the truth and excluded from the rest of the family, for example by being sent away to relatives or back to school at the time of the funeral, are likely to become bewildered, frightened or resentful. Children make up what they don't know, and their imaginings are usually worse than the truth. Silence to a child may well feed the fantasy that she is to blame for the death. Silence will certainly risk a loss of trust between adult and child.

It is, of course, impossible not to communicate with children. They are adept at picking up atmospheres and feelings, and they will instinctively understand if the adults around them do not want to talk or show their feelings. Adults often assume it is they who are protecting children from anxieties, when it is children who protect adults from the upset, which feels more frightening when shrouded in mystery. So what do children need to help address their anxieties?

The commonest anxieties experienced by children relate to:

- *responsibility*: Was it my fault? Did I somehow cause the death? Could I have done anything to stop it happening? Why him and not me?
- *mortality*: Will I die too? Am I at risk? Will it be my turn next? Who else will die?
- *security*: Who will look out for me now? How will I keep safe? What will happen? Am I still loved and accepted?

Such concerns may be verbalised, though more commonly they are expressed in physical and behavioural reactions, particularly in younger children. These may include:

- anxiety about being separated from parents or carers
- difficulty in going to sleep, or fear of the dark
- regressing to an earlier stage, such as clinging, bedwetting or baby talk
- a tendency to infections
- reluctance to go to school
- difficulty in concentrating
- over-eating, or conversely losing interest in food
- developing a phobia about doctors or hospitals
- angry and aggressive outbursts
- becoming withdrawn and depressed.

These are normal reactions and most will pass with time. Meanwhile there are some practical responses which can be put in place, such as providing a nightlight, but in general the overwhelming need is for understanding and reassurance. At a time of bewilderment and upheaval, the child needs to be held emotionally and perhaps physically too.

First principles

These are becoming clear from the above consideration of what we observe and what children themselves report of their bereavement experiences. So far we have identified the common needs of children for:

- information and explanation about the illness, death, funeral etc
- inclusion and involvement in discussions, plans, decisions, rituals
- understanding and reassurance about their feelings and concerns.

It follows that the adults seeking to meet these needs require a level of openness, warmth and honesty in communicating with children. It may also take courage.

Who is best placed to talk with the child?

Obviously the parents are ideally suited to meet the needs and conditions listed above. When that is not possible, it should be a known and trusted adult, who has an ongoing relationship with the child. Other family members or close friends may help out if the parent is in extreme distress. Parents who are in shock, or absorbed with practical tasks around the time of the death, may need some prompting and guidance from concerned professionals: 'Have you thought what you are going to say to his sister?' Later, it's helpful for parents and teachers to discuss what the child has been told and how the death is experienced or understood within the family's culture and belief systems.

When to talk?

The simple answer is, as soon as possible. When it comes to giving bad news or information about the death, any delay makes it more likely that the child will be told by the wrong person in an unhelpful way. The child has to know eventually and may misinterpret any delay or avoidance as indicating some fault or blame attached to herself. At the very least, delay suggests disinterest, and risks isolating the child from the rest of the family.

Timing is not so obvious when the adult is concerned to give the child an opportunity to express and explore her reactions, and to open up a dialogue. Then it may be better to make spaces and times which encourage open communication, such as bathtime, bedtime, storytime, walking the dog together, asking for help with a task. Familiarity with the child and sensitivity to her temperament will then determine whether it is better to initiate the dialogue, or offer some cues to signal your willingness to listen, or simply wait for the child to talk when ready.

How to communicate with children and young people

In his introduction to his book *Talking About Death*, Earl Grollman offers this advice:

> 'Approach the discussion gently and lovingly; the tone of your voice should be warm, sympathetic, kind. *What* is said is significant, but *how* you say it will have a greater bearing on whether youngsters develop morbid fears or will be able to accept, within their capacity, the reality of death.'

Grollman also reminds us to go at the child's pace. Young children particularly need time to absorb information and time to come back to their feelings and queries, perhaps after some distracting play between.

The following guidelines on communicating with children build on the experience of Barbara Monroe at St Christopher's Hospice and other people working with bereaved children and families.

- *Talk at eye level*. This is fundamental. It signals interest and a willingness to engage in a real dialogue with the child. It creates the right conditions for reading body language, picking up clues, and responding in a respectful way. It facilitates touching and hold-ing (if appropriate). It is non-threatening and non-patronising.

- *Speak directly to and with the child.* This may seem obvious, but at stressful times it's all too easy for adults – particularly professionals – to speak to the child through another adult.
- *Avoid confusing and ambivalent language.* Examples are legion and legendary: 'We have lost your brother/He has gone to sleep forever/He has passed away.' The corollary advice is not to be afraid to use the words 'death', 'dying' and 'dead'.
- *Avoid cliches and platitudes.* These readily spring to the lips when anxious to protect or reassure the child: 'Perhaps it's for the best/The good die young.' Such phrases are no help to the child and only serve to protect the adult from the discomfort of facing reality.
- *Keep explanations short and simple.* Be prepared to repeat ex-planations, perhaps in different ways. Link observations to what the child already knows and what she has experienced. Ask what she thinks and feels. Use the images she offers.
- *Check the child's understanding.* Grollman tells a lovely story of how we need to check that the meaning of the speaker meets the understanding of the listener:

'I was once asked by a young girl, "How long is death?" I responded, "Death is permanent." The youngster said, "Oh, then it's not so bad." Noticing my bewilderment she said simply, "My mother has permanents at the hairdresser. It doesn't last very long".'

Grollman, 1990

Even simple words can be misunderstood. A friend of mine grasped the nettle when her little boy asked what had happened to his friend after he had died. She explained how the body was washed and dressed; how the body would be placed in the coffin; and even what would happen to the body after burial. His puzzled look was explained by his next question: 'And what happens to the head?'

- *Be truthful and honest.* The cost of hiding or avoiding the truth is to lose the trust of the child. Children are amazingly resilient and often surprise us by their ability to handle difficult information. There is a caveat to this guideline, of course, which is to use language appropriate to the child's age and ability. Being honest may involve answering difficult questions with 'I don't know' or 'I'm not sure' or 'I'll come back to you on that when I've had time to think'. Honesty may also mean owning your feelings: 'I am hurt/angry/puzzled too.'
- *Keep them informed.* Tell the child what has happened/is happening and what will happen next. Prepare her for changes in others and herself.
- *Keep the dialogue open.* This does not mean pushing the child to talk, but being aware of the child's need to revisit their reactions to the death in the future, as well as the special effect of anniversaries and significant life changes.

Finally, a reminder that there are more questions than answers. It is more important to listen to a child's concerns and to show you have heard them, than to meet questions with 'right' answers.

Helping children understand about terminal illness

Children who have lived with a sibling's chronic illness will be used to the stresses and strains that it brings for all family members. They may experience frequent separations from the sick sibling when hospitalised and indeed from parents. Inevitably parents have less time and energy to spend with their well children, and daily routines are disrupted. Well children may not, however, understand that the illness is life-threatening, or that the ill child will die (even when the outcome is obvious to the adult) unless they are prepared. Preparation is also needed for changes in the sick child's condition and whatever consequences may follow.

What about the direct question, 'Is he going to die?' Anticipating such a question, perhaps with the support of another adult, can help the parent or professional prepare a response which manages to balance realism with hope, such as, 'I hope he won't die, but he is very poorly, and the doctor says he might not get better.'

Children are helped by the adults around them talking to each other. There are obvious benefits to children in maintaining school routines and out-of-school activities, and when teachers and club leaders are kept informed of what is happening in the family, they can respond in a helpful way.

Teenagers are particularly vulnerable as they get caught up in the ambivalent feelings of adolescence. They may swing from wanting to take on an adult helping role, to being resentful of disruption to their normal life. Teenagers may be less likely to initiate discussion with adults, turning more naturally to friends, but they are still in need of up-to-date information and the opportunities to talk. Some find that talking is easier with teachers, doctors and nurses than with parents.

Informing children of the death

Faced with such a difficult task, you may need to deal with your own anxieties first. Talking it through with a friend or colleague can help to clarify what needs to be said and what may get in the way of saying it. Apart from any practical problems regarding the time and place, it will be your feelings which will cause concern: embarrassment; fear of the child's distress; fear of becoming upset yourself; wanting to get it right; and feeling clumsy and helpless. Naming and facing those feelings can go a good way towards reducing their impact.

As part of your preparation you may find it useful to rehearse what you are going to say, either verbally or in writing. How this is done will depend on the situation.

- In one-to-one meetings with a child, you can access *more* spontaneity and sincerity by having considered the options beforehand and then putting them out of your mind, trusting to the moment.
- In situations where your task is to address a group of children, you are well advised to have a crib sheet of the points you want to cover, to ensure they are not lost as the interactive group process unfolds.
- If several adults are going to speak to several groups concurrently, as may happen in larger schools, it makes sense for a prepared script to be available. This ensures consistency, that the same information is received by different groups. It also helps those who are feeling diffident and ill-equipped, as the script can be read or adapted to the individual's style. Some schools which have faced this situation have put in extra helpers, such as volunteer parents or classroom assistants, to support or share the teacher's task.

A prepared script might go something like this:

'I want you all to listen carefully as I have some very sad news to tell you, which might upset you. Some of you may already have heard that Jan was knocked down by a car yesterday evening while he was out on his bike. He was badly injured and was taken to hospital. He had an operation and the doctors tried very hard to save his life. Sadly he was too badly hurt to recover, and he died in the early hours of this morning. His mum and dad have sent a message to say that they are not sure how it happened, but they think Jan lost control of his bike coming down the hill near his house, and swerved into the path of a car which couldn't stop in time. Jan was knocked out and did not regain consciousness, so although he was badly injured, he didn't feel any pain. That's all we know at the moment. Later there will be a public report called an inquest, which will investigate how and why he died. There will be a funeral some time next week, and Jan's family would like

> the school to be involved somehow. I will let you know as soon as the school has further information about that.'

Such a script offers a form of words which may be used, but more importantly it covers the essential elements for enabling the expression of grief:

- what happened
- how it happened
- why it happened
- what happens next.

These components help the child confront the reality of the death and begin to try and make some sense of it. A base has been established for the expression of the child's reactions and the asking of questions, and time needs to be made available for this. Children of all ages, and particularly younger children, welcome the opportunity to move on to practical tasks and plans to focus their energy, such as a card, collage, poem, memory corner or website.

In summary, a checklist of breaking sad news to children follows the same principles as the guidelines on breaking bad news at the beginning of Chapter 5.

- **Why?**   Because otherwise the child will get to know in less desirable ways.

    To engender trust and to facilitate the healthy expression of grief.
- **When?**   As soon as possible.
- **By whom?**   By someone known and trusted by the child(ren).
- **Where?**   In familiar, safe and comfortable surroundings.
- **How?**   In a straightforward and unambiguous way, in language which is easily understood, with sensitivity,

with time and opportunity to express feelings and ask questions.

Finally, get support for yourself. It is just as important to have the support of that friend or colleague afterwards to pick up on how it went and how you are left feeling.

Telling children about a murder or suicide

'I knew she was missing but they didn't tell me anything else …
the way I found out she was murdered was from the television.
It was like they couldn't be bothered to tell me.'

It is easy to understand the bewilderment and hurt of this young teenager whose older sister was murdered. But imagine also the shocked state of her parents at the time, unable to bring themselves to tell their younger daughter what they did not want to believe themselves. It's easy with hindsight to see the folly of trying to protect her from the truth for as long as possible. Even a few minutes' reflection will show up the blind spot in this logic. Of course the surviving siblings, and other children, will get to know the circumstances of the death, sooner or later, from children in the playground, from overhearing adults or through the media. And the more sensational the cause of death, notably murder or suicide, the more likely it is that rumour and fantasy will distort the truth. Another few minutes' reflection serves to remind us that when children learn that they were not told the truth, they are commonly led to one of two conclusions: that they cannot trust those adults in the future; or that they must somehow be to blame, and that's why they were not told.

It's hard enough for us as adults to come to terms with such destructive acts as the murder or suicide of a child without the added burden of telling other children. So here again the starting point is to pay attention to your own reactions, even if you have to put them on hold for the time being while you address immediate tasks. Give yourself some breathing space to discuss with a colleague, or consult with a specialist, how you are going to tackle this delicate subject with the child(ren) in your care.

Younger children may well need help with understanding new words such as murder, manslaughter, homicide, suicide, overdose etc. The more difficult task is to help them with the concepts behind the words. How can we understand the murder of a child, or the self-destructive act of a young person?

A second but separate issue is how much detail to include in the telling. Is it (a) necessary and (b) appropriate to say how the young person was murdered or how he took his own life? If you had the task of communicating such news to primary school classes, what would you say to Year Six children that you wouldn't say to Year One children (who may have siblings in Year Six)?

More questions than answers, and each one needing careful consideration. These are also times for trusting that your own sincerity and compassion will be understood and respected by even very young children, even when you are struggling for words.

The following vignettes are offered for consideration, one the murder of a seven-year-old girl, and the other the suicide of a 16-year-old boy. Both are based on true stories but hopefully disguised beyond recognition.

Esther's murder

Esther, aged seven, went missing on a Thursday and on Saturday her naked body was found on waste ground a mile from her home. A post-mortem held on Sunday revealed that she had been sexually assaulted and had died from head injuries. The same day a young man was arrested and charged with her murder.

The headteacher of the school attended by Esther and her five-year-old sister faced the dilemma of what to say to the children on Monday. The night before she consulted with her deputy, the police, the chair of governors, Esther's parents, and other parents. She decided to use the same form of words with each class in turn:

'I have something to say to you which is very sad and hard to understand. Some of you know that Esther was missing last Thursday and no-one could find her. Everyone was very worried. I went to see her mother and father on Friday, and they were upset because they did not know what had happened or where she was. Then on Saturday a policeman came to see me and told me that something really bad had happened to Esther. A woman walking her dog found Esther lying in some long grass. But she wasn't moving or breathing because she was dead. The police took her body to the hospital for some tests. The tests showed that Esther had died because someone had killed her. This is called murder. Esther had been injured/hurt in different parts of her body, but the injuries to her head were the ones which killed her. That means we can hope she died quickly and didn't feel much hurt.

The police think they have caught the man who did this to Esther, but they don't know for sure. They will keep this man in prison until the case comes to court in a few months' time, so we don't have to worry about that.

It's hard to understand why anyone should want to hurt and kill Esther. Some people say that this man must be bad, and some say he must be mad. It's rare for a murder to happen. Most people grow old without knowing anyone who has been murdered but they might read about it in the paper or hear about it on the news.'

What would *you* have said?

Jordan's suicide

At the age of 16 Jordan rarely attended school and supported his increasing drug use with odd jobs and petty theft. In spite of a bravado exterior, he experienced black moods. His relationship with his parents was stormy and he frequently 'left home' to stay with other family members. So a note he left for his mum after the last argument saying 'I am going for good this time' was not taken too seriously. When he was found hanged in a disused barn it seemed impossible to draw any other conclusion than that he intended to take his own life. The post-mortem showed a cocktail of drugs present in his body, including hallucinogenic substances.

After consultation, the headteacher scripted the following statement for form tutors:

> 'This is a very sad day for the school. Many of you will have heard the tragic news of Jordan's death. I want to tell you what happened, with the agreement of Jordan's family, to avoid rumour and speculation. We know how he died. We know that he hanged himself, which means he probably died instantly. We don't know why he died. As you know, when someone ends their own life, this is called suicide. It's very difficult to understand why anyone should want to kill themselves. It's rare, and it usually happens when someone is extremely confused or depressed, much worse than the normal feelings of being mixed up or fed up that most people have from time to time. We do know that Jordan was under the influence of drugs when he died, but we don't know how much the drugs affected his state of mind. It's important not to guess or make assumptions, even if we knew Jordan well. It is the job of the inquest, which is an official enquiry, to look at all the evidence as to how and why Jordan died.'

Would you phrase this differently? What else would you say?

Summary of dos and don'ts

Do aim for dialogue, rather than talking at children.
Do practise using the 'death' word and talking about death as a fact of life.

Do remember the importance of information and involvement for children.

Do prepare yourself and what you are going to say.

Do allow for a child's expression of grief, and for a child's questions.

Do allow yourself to show your feelings.

Do seek consultation and support for yourself.

Don't use stories and fairy tales to explain the mystery of death.

Don't make out that you have all the answers.

Don't leave room for a child's wondering whether she might have been to blame.

Don't underestimate your ability to help a child by listening and showing you care.

References

Gold A and Yule W (1993) *Wise Before the Event*. Calouste Gulbenkian Foundation.

Grollman EA (1990) *Talking About Death: a dialogue between parent and child*. Beacon Press, Boston.

Hindmarch C (1995) Secondary losses for siblings. *Child: care, health and development*. **21**(6): 425–31. Blackwell Science Ltd.

Turner M (1998) *Talking with Children and Young People about Death and Dying*. Jessica Kingsley Publishers, London.

Winston's Wish booklet *Supporting a Child who is Bereaved through Suicide* (*see* Appendix A for address).

Section 3

Bereavement support

7 Support for families

'Hope is incredible to the prisoner of grief.'

Petrarch

The kind of support offered should ideally be determined by the needs of the bereaved, but realistically it will also depend on what resources are available. Different models for support services will be considered in the final chapter, but first it is necessary to describe the various approaches and what they aim to achieve. Other questions addressed are:

- how and when is this strategy appropriate?
- who offers this kind of help?
- how can this support be obtained?

Practical support

In the early days there is usually a need for practical support, particularly in the case of sudden death. Parents in extreme shock may find themselves unable to care adequately for their other children. They may find it hard to sleep, or to think about food, or to apply themselves to the practical arrangements that need to be made. The offer of a lift or childminding or the gift of a casserole can convey as much comfort as any words.

Ideally this kind of practical help is forthcoming from extended family, friends and neighbours who are sensitive to the parents' needs. However, not all parents want relief from practical tasks and would prefer to be busy doing things as a way of coping with the pain. It needs to be their choice. If in doubt, ask them. There is no virtue in guessing, although there is often an expectation that one should know what is best for other people!

Well-meaning relatives may be overzealous in their concern to protect their loved ones. An obvious example is the tendency for brothers and sisters of the dying or dead child being bundled away from the scene of action. Even at a very young age children will experience a sense of exclusion if they are 'sent away' at such a time. They may then feel somehow punished and guilty, but are likely to comply with the expectations of the adults around them that they should play nicely and not ask questions. Children learn quickly to protect their protectors. On the other hand, some children may be very relieved to have some respite from distress, and welcome the chance to stay with a favourite aunt for a break.

How does one know which course is preferred by a particular child? Ask the child. Even very young children, once freed of responsibility for 'looking after' their parents, know what they want and can be trusted to know what is right for them. If the possible alternatives are openly offered, for example 'Do you want to stay here with Mummy and Daddy tonight, or do you want to stay the night with Granny?', most children will give a truthful answer. As well as getting it right for the child, it is equally important to the child that she has been asked.

An example of well-meaning relatives not taking account of a parent's wishes is given here by Joyce:

'I was 19 and unmarried when I had my first baby, and that was seen as a disgrace in those days. It was the year of the Aberfan tragedy. Catherine was born with the cord round her neck and she only lived 10 minutes. Somebody said: "It's the best thing that could have happened". There were complications so I had to stay in hospital for two weeks. My mum saw to the funeral and I only found out later where the baby was buried. The worst was when I got home: my mum had given everything away that I'd got ready for the baby – cot, pram, clothes, the lot. I know she thought she was doing it for the best, but I had nothing tangible left to connect with the baby and what I'd lost, nothing to grieve with.'

Not everyone has a good network of family support to fall back on. When this is the case, key community figures such as the clergy, church visitor or social worker will assume more significance in providing practical help. Where several people are involved it is obviously important to co-ordinate efforts and to work co-operatively. The family doctor might most naturally take on this co-ordinating role, although it could just as easily be the health visitor or social worker.

Whatever the role, any visitor to the home of a bereaved family is likely to feel apprehensive – may actually be terrified – about the level of distress within, and conscious of not knowing what to say or do to help. It takes courage to make the first call. However, having made contact, it is important only to offer support that can realistically be maintained.

Befriending

Several of the specialist support organisations, such as the Foundation for the Study of Infant Deaths, the Scottish Cot Death Trust, and The Compassionate Friends provide a valuable befriending service. More generally, The Samaritans may offer face-to-face contact as well as 24-hour crisis support by telephone. Hospices and church visitor schemes, and victim support organisations may also offer a befriending service.

Befriending is rather like a one-way friendship. The helper offers the acceptance and listening ear of a friend without the emotional ties which require mutuality. Talking has many therapeutic effects:

- it helps to accept the reality of the loss
- it is a way of expressing and discharging emotions

- it helps to normalise reactions
- it re-establishes order to a disorganised mind.

Most bereaved parents experience the need to go over and over the events surrounding the death and to talk about the baby or child in every detail. This can become wearing for relatives and friends. Not everyone is as fortunate as Rose:

> 'My sister and brother-in-law visited every evening from the day Paul was killed in September to Christmas. It was the highlight of my day, knowing that Betty was coming round and I could just be myself and talk about Paul.'

Jo and John faced a more usual situation:

> 'Our families and friends were very supportive at first, but after a few weeks, although people still asked how we were, nobody mentioned *David* any more, when we wanted to talk about him more than ever.'

Having permission and encouragement to talk are crucially important to all bereaved, and the more so when the bereavement is a social embarrassment. Giving that permission and encouragement are key tasks for befrienders. Their value should not be underestimated and this usually voluntary role can be difficult. It demands witnessing another's pain, being faced with unanswerable questions and being left with feelings of helplessness and inadequacy.

Preparation

Ideally the helper will have received some training in listening skills and at least some preparation for the implications of the role. The conditions of the befriending relationship need to be thought through beforehand regarding availability and expectations. Where does the contact take place? How long should one stay on a home visit? Is a home telephone number to be given out? The befriender will need support, and should not be left to ask for it if feeling under pressure. A built-in support system is the best way to ensure that the expectations of the role do not become overwhelming.

Who should take on this role?

As in other situations of adversity and trauma, one naturally turns to someone who has suffered a similar experience. There is a common bond which is conducive to trust and understanding. Therefore bereaved parents will often seek out contact with other parents to gain reassurance that they are not alone and that they can survive their tragedy.

If this support is being offered by bereaved parents, they obviously need to have reached the point where they can keep their own grief separate when in this role. Nevertheless it is likely that their own grief will at times be re-awakened by another's pain, which again underlines the necessity for support.

Whether or not the befriender has lost a child, there is one golden rule: never to say, 'I know exactly how you feel'. This ranks as the cardinal sin of all platitudes. It robs the sufferer of the uniqueness of the individual experience.

When is befriending appropriate?

There is no prescribed time or circumstance, but the following could be taken as indicators.

- When the parent is not able to offload to family or friends.
- When the early support of family and friends has fallen off.
- When the parent is isolated or housebound.
- When the parent is struggling with the task of adjustment, practically or emotionally.
- When the parent is confronting difficult times such as an inquest, birthday, Christmas, anniversary.

Points to consider

- Is befriending appropriate?
- Is there a suitable helper available?
- Are the conditions of the relationship clear?
- Is there sufficient support for the befriender?

Counselling

Counselling has taken on a variety of meanings for different people, ranging from advice to long-term therapy. Basic assumptions are that counselling will provide *help* for someone with a *problem*, and that a trained counsellor will have the necessary *skills*. Referrals are often made by other professionals who feel out of their depth and lack the competency required.

It seems important to examine these assumptions in an attempt to clarify the role of the bereavement counsellor and to arrive at some indicators as to when counselling is appropriate.

The purpose of counselling

In many contexts counselling is seen as a problem-solving activity, with the counsellor guiding the client towards resolution of the problem. This idea does not fit comfortably with bereavement, and yet the expectation of both client and referrer is often that the bereavement counsellor will do or say something to make things better. In fact, the focus of the work in all therapeutic counselling is with the client, who sets the pace and the agenda. A more useful view of bereavement counselling is that it provides a means of expressing grief and working on the tasks of mourning. For some, this may be the opportunity to deal with suppressed feelings of anger and despair. For others, bereavement will turn their world upside down in such a way that all areas of life are called into question – relationships, job, religion – and huge adjustments are required.

The following comment comes from a staff counsellor:

'I have recently had two clients who had lost children through short illnesses. Both of them said that the counselling sessions were like "touching base" in a frightening, changed world, and felt they had benefitted from this. I guess they're expressing a sort of "normalising" in an abnormal world.'

The loss of a child questions the meaning of life in a way that few would otherwise face. The loss of a child also contains a very special ingredient: that this child could have been the receiver and giver of the unconditional love we all crave. Thus, the counselling relationship may be instrumental in rebuilding self-esteem and self-worth. The bereavement counsellor may become, for a while, the ideal parent we all wished we had and would like to be for our children.

The tasks of counselling

Grief counselling, then, may include any of the following tasks:

- believing the reality of the loss
- experiencing the pain of that loss
- adjusting to daily existence without the loved child
- making sense of a world that allowed such a tragic waste
- working out one's future direction and reason for living.

This was Barbara's experience:

'What brought me to counselling? I just seemed to be caught up in a dense fog which I could not escape from and at times this left me feeling totally lost and almost blind with panic. Counselling helped me to clear the fog and find the sky – even though the sky is still cloudy at times. Counselling has enabled me to sort through my jumbled experiences and feelings and recognise each for what it was. By recognising these things I could deal with those that could be dealt with and learn to live with those that I cannot do anything about. Initially, it helped me to put some perspective into my life. I realised that I was not the only mother to have lost a baby. I directed my thoughts to one issue at a time and gradually I got some sense of control in my life. It has proved to be very liberating.'

The role of the counsellor

It follows from the above that the role of the bereavement counsellor is a demanding one and requires more than the use of counselling skills practised by many other helpers in the course of their work. This distinction is not a judgment of value, nor does it deny the competence of professionals who take on a counselling role without that 'specialist' job title. Indeed, there are many who by nature of their existing professional relationship with the bereaved, such as the GP, health visitor or social worker, are best placed to take it on. However, it is important to be clear about what the role requires and involves. It is misleading and irresponsible when people are described or describe themselves as bereavement counsellors on the basis of goodwill and a day's training in counselling skills. What, then, are the requirements for this role?

- Counsellors need to have done sufficient work on their own losses to be aware of their impact on their counselling.
- Counsellors need a level of training that has developed understanding of attachment and loss, the features of grief, the tasks of mourning and of the processes at work in the therapeutic relationship.
- Counsellors need a setting that gives clear boundaries to the work – a counselling 'contract' – particularly if they have other roles in relation to the client or patient.
- Counsellors need supervision to clarify the task in hand and to cope with the emotional demands and feelings of helplessness.

- Counsellors need the knowledge and assessment skills required to recognise the relevance of grief reactions to the presentation of depression and anxiety states.

When is counselling appropriate?

As counselling is here defined as more in-depth than listening, more focused and detached than befriending, it follows that it is not appropriate in the early days of grief, not until the first traumatic shock-waves from the diagnosis or from the actual death have subsided. It would be like starting physiotherapy straight after breaking a leg, instead of allowing time for the initial healing to take place. It may be helpful to pursue this analogy, as not everyone needs physiotherapy after breaking a leg. With good health, good healing and good support one can learn to walk again unaided. However, if there are other injuries, if the healing is complicated, or if insufficient attention and time are given to the healing before weight-bearing, it is a different story. Similarly, the painful experience of losing a child may be complicated by particularly traumatic circumstances. It may re-awaken the pain of previous losses, losses that perhaps have not been acknowledged or resolved. Other demands of family or job may not allow time and opportunity to grieve, so that the painful feelings become suppressed. In these situations, the focused attention afforded by counselling can help to release the blockages to natural healing.

There are also special features associated with the loss of a child which may complicate grieving and may indicate a need of counselling. One such feature is the fear of insanity, which many parents experience. The frightening and unrelenting extremity of emotions, together with the inability to make sense of what has happened, can send the mind into chaos. Another common experience is feeling suicidal, sometimes driven by guilt, sometimes by a desire to be with the dead baby or child. These reactions are isolating and put a tremendous strain on relationships, between spouses, partners and with other family members. The counselling setting can provide a place of safety to discharge these tensions.

Counselling is an obvious resource when chronic grief reactions are manifested in depression, anxiety states, panic attacks and phobic reactions. Family members may present with such symptoms years after the bereavement, and commonly a sensitive GP will make the connection and refer for counselling, perhaps alongside medication. Counselling, as a talking therapy, offers a safe and structured environment for the client to revisit the traumatic losses underlying their symptoms. The counselling relationship is formalised in a 'contract', i.e. an agreement to work together in clearly defined conditions as to time and place and purpose. Counselling methods will depend on the therapeutic approach favoured by the counsellor, and should also be guided by the client's needs. People who need help in expressing emotions will obviously benefit from a counselling method which focuses on feelings; while those who want to find new meaning and direction in their lives will be better suited to a cognitive approach. The same person may benefit from these different methods at different times, requiring the counsellor to adapt to whatever mode is suitable for the task in hand. Whatever the approach, the most important ingredient is the *therapeutic relationship* between counsellor and client which hopefully provides the medium for the selected method to become effective.

The duration of counselling will depend on various factors. It could be said that bereavement does not fit easily with short-term approaches like solution-focused brief therapy, because the central task is not to focus on solutions to problems. However, it may be enough to learn some strategies for coping with new realities. Bereavement counselling may be sought at a time when the client is preparing for a transition to another stage in post-bereavement adjustment, and so may have fulfilled its purpose when, say, a bereaved father is re-established at work, or a bereaved mother is pregnant again. On the other hand, it could be precisely at this time that the newly pregnant woman experiences a *greater* need for counselling – particularly if the death was of a baby – so perhaps the real message here is not to make assumptions. Counselling in response to what may be regarded as complicated grief reactions is more likely to be long term, maybe lasting more than a year. In reality the number of sessions may depend on resources and whether limits are imposed by the funders. Counselling from a private practitioner may offer more flexibility but will depend on ability to pay.

For more on different aspects of bereavement counselling and when it is appropriate, see *Gift of Tears* by Lendrum and Syme (1992).

How is bereavement counselling different from other counselling?

Bereavement counsellors are sometimes referred to as a special breed. In fact the title simply denotes a chosen area of specialism, and all counsellors will deal with bereavement to a lesser or greater degree. It could even be said that the issue of loss is central to all counselling. Having said that, there are some strategies which are associated with grief work, particularly to facilitate the expression of grief in situations where the mourner feels 'stuck'. Such strategies include the following:

- The use of photographs, videos and memorabilia as sensory triggers to access emotional memory.
- The construction of geneograms to identify patterns of loss and other affective factors in the family.
- The use of the written word, both in the reading of literature and poetry, and through the client's own writings.
- The use of drawing and painting in free expression which bypasses the need for words and helps to access feelings more directly.
- In vivo work, i.e. the revisiting of the scene of the death, the hospital where the death occurred, the grave, or other significant places. This may be done by the client alone, with others, or with the counsellor.

- The use of letters, tapes or 'empty chair' work, to help the client deal with 'unfinished business' – to express unspoken thoughts and feelings to the person who has died.
- Helping the client to devise and carry out personalised rituals to say goodbye or commemorate the life/death. This may be useful when the mourner has for some reason missed the funeral.
- Working with the whole family, perhaps in conjunction with another counsellor. This may be particularly appropriate regarding child loss, to avoid the false separation of issues and exclusion of some family members, usually siblings.

Some of these techniques are very powerful and should only be used when the counsellor has experienced them first-hand in the training setting, and can discuss their application in supervision.

Where should counselling take place?

The usual setting is a designated space in the counsellor's consulting rooms or the health practice, hospital or organisation where the counsellor works. This affords privacy, freedom from interruption, standard conditions and safety for both parties. It denotes a special time and place for the client and the client's changing relationship with the dead child. Coming to the counsellor may also be seen as a test of commitment to engaging with painful feelings and difficult issues which arise. All these factors have contributed to the view that counselling in the client's home is second best, where the counselling may be subject to distractions such as pets, visitors and other family members. On the other hand, home visits offer many bonuses. The client is seen in context, in terms of family and culture. The client may have more confidence in familiar surroundings, feel more in control of a new experience; and some might only engage in counselling on home ground. Above all, the home visit may indicate respect for the dead child in the place where he once lived and to the family holding his memory. In this regard office consultations are no substitute for home visits.

Certainly, counselling in the home requires more flexibility from the counsellor as well as secure boundaries. Where there is a choice, the pros and cons would need to be considered as part of ongoing assessment and supervision.

Availability of counselling

The first consideration is whether there is someone already involved and acceptable to the bereaved person who can meet the criteria given above, in terms of having awareness, training, time and supervision. If so, it is important that the counselling is set up separately from other activities, and has clear time limits. If these conditions are not met, it may be difficult for both to cope with the painful feelings aroused. Professionals for whom counselling is a secondary role will arrange to see someone at a time set aside for addressing the bereavement issues.

More and more health practices are employing trained counsellors, reflecting a more holistic approach to health and greater under-standing of the relationship between emotional and physical well being. In some parts of the UK there are bereavement centres or services with counsellors who have particular experience of working with grief. This was how Pam came to counselling:

'I lost my son 12 years ago. I thought I was managing OK but after a few years I was back and forth to the doctor with one thing and another – pains across my shoulders, down my back, stomach ache … He was very good: in the end he said that either I went to a counsellor or he wouldn't be my GP any more! So I had no choice, though I didn't see it would do any good. In fact once I got there I realised how much I had been holding in and how much I needed to talk about my feelings. I grieved in a way I hadn't allowed myself to do before. I still need to talk about Simon from time to time. If I don't, the feelings come from nowhere and hit me in the back of the neck.'

Where a referral system operates, it is important that the bereaved person is encouraged to self-refer, as it could be that a third party referral is more about the referrer's anxiety to help than the bereaved person's wish to be helped. Similarly, response to referrals should be directly with the bereaved, and thought given to how much information, if any, is shared with other professionals.

Where to refer?

Whatever the setting, how can the credibility and suitability of the counsellor be checked? Every counsellor, whether self-appointed or working within an organisation, should be able to provide the enquirer with information about their code of ethics, training and ways of working.

Checklist of indicators for counselling

So many factors affect the course of grieving that it is impossible to predict who might benefit from counselling. However, here are some of the indicators:

- low self-esteem
- persistent suicidal feelings
- breakdown of relationships
- multiple or coincidental losses
- traumatic circumstances surrounding the death.

Psychotherapy

The distinction between counselling and therapy is a fine one. In the USA the words 'therapy' and 'therapist' are more or less synonymous with 'counselling' and 'counsellor' in the UK. To add to the confusion, some counsellors in the UK describe themselves as psychotherapists on the grounds that they are doing the same work.

What, then, is the difference? In terms of training, the psycho-therapist is required to have undergone individual or group therapy and will have access to the psychodynamic approach, which facilitates the resolution of underlying conflicts of separation, probably from childhood. The psychotherapist is likely to work actively with the tranference of feelings that occur in the therapeutic relationship. Anyone with deep-seated personality problems would be better suited to this psychodynamic approach. The psychotherapist may use specialist techniques belonging to a particular school of therapy.

At the same time, some trained counsellors will use the same assessment skills and range of techniques. This is a welcome reflection of the rising standards of professionalism in the counselling world. Unfortunately it leaves blurred edges between these two definitions and uncertainty about who to go to when more in-depth work is required. Reference to the British Association for Counselling Directory of Counsellors and Therapists may be helpful.

Psychology

Further distinctions need to be made for those seeking specialist help.

Generally speaking, referrals to a psychologist focus on behavioural concerns. The behavioural approach may be indicated for someone whose bereavement has led to entrenched phobic reactions, such as the panic attacks associated with agoraphobia. Whilst the training for clinical psychology is traditionally behavioural in origin, the psychologist is not restricted to this approach. Referrals are assessed individually and the appropriate therapy is offered. Where children are concerned, this may take the form of play therapy, or work with the whole family. Referral to a clinical psychologist can be made through the GP or, in some cases, directly to the psychology service at the hospital.

When the help of a child psychologist is engaged for grieving siblings who show distressing and persistent behavioural changes, it is essential that such help is seen by the child as supportive. Otherwise there is the real danger that the child is scapegoated for the parents' or family's difficulties and will be labelled as a 'problem'.

Psychiatry

Traditional psychiatric support is seen to be appropriate in the context of mental illness, and concentrates on drug treatments. Although many bereaved parents do, for a time, experience mental chaos and fear they are going mad, this is different from the long-term separation from reality that accompanies psychotic illness. Also, the depression which normally accompanies bereavement – the suppressing of painful feelings – needs to be distinguished from depressive illness, which is physically dysfunctional and requires medical treatment.

However, in some hospitals and child guidance centres, psychiatrists who work alongside psychologists and social workers offer a more flexible response and make use of other therapeutic skills. This multidisciplinary approach is also commonly used for family therapy. This may be the desired option when the death of a child results in family dysfunction. It has obvious advantages when one member of the family – usually another child – is carrying responsibility for all the family's distress. The desired outcome of involving all or some of the family members is to help each one acknowledge feelings and be acknowledged – thus helping the family adjust to its loss. Family therapy may be available through the local health services, social services and voluntary agencies such as Barnardo's and the Children's Society.

Finally, a word about the value of these different therapeutic approaches. It is hard to get away from the assumption that those practitioners who have had more specialised training and are better paid also offer 'better' services. However, the worth of any counselling or therapy depends on the *quality* of the attention given to the bereaved person or family.

The word therapist comes from the ancient Greek 'therapon', a servant who freely chose to devote his life to giving attention to others' needs. To make the same point in another way, as the antipsychiatrist RD Laing said, 'Treatment is about how you treat people'. The core qualities of warmth, empathy and respect form the basis of any supportive relationship. Carol found just these qualities in her befriender:

> 'Jenny saw me through the worst time, really. For the first months after James died I couldn't go out, not even to the shops. I felt I couldn't face anyone. I rang a helpline one evening, and after that Jenny came to see me every week till I got my confidence back. She knew just what I was going through, because she'd been there too. And I remember thinking, she's survived, so maybe I will.'

Groups

Meeting together with others to form a group is a powerful experience. This is particularly true for those who feel isolated by the shattering effects of losing a child. Common bonds are formed by that shared experience which cuts across differences in age, social status, education and religion. It can be enormously reassuring and enabling to hear others express similar thoughts and feelings, and to know they face similar difficulties. It can provide a safe environment for dropping the public mask of normality and owning inner struggles with pain, anger, guilt and frustration. Negatives are balanced by positives, so that one member can feed off another's hope or optimism.

Lin's daughter Yvonne, aged 15, was killed in a road accident while on holiday abroad. These are her recollections about attending a parents' group:

'It saved my sanity. I felt very lonely, and I used to feel as if I was going mad, talking to Yvonne as if she was still in the house; but when I heard others say similar things, I thought 'Thank God, it happens to them too'. I felt I could just be *me* there, whether in a happy mood or at rock bottom. I could laugh without feeling apologetic, and cry without feeling ashamed.'

Groups can also be extremely threatening for the same reason, that shared feelings are intensified. For some, particularly in the early days of bereavement, it is just too much to consider anyone else's pain but one's own. Timing and preparation are therefore important for anyone joining a group. The nature of the group will also affect the outcome. Does it have a therapeutic purpose, or is it focused on shared activities? Is it exclusive to parents, to adults, or to families? Are affected children to be offered a separate group? Some children's bereavement projects have discovered the benefit of running two separate groups for children and their parents/carers at the same time.

Self-help groups

The main focus of the self-help group is mutual support. The structure is usually informal and the agenda set by the members. It often provides a network of support outside the group meetings, leading to new friendships. Although there is freedom from the leadership of outside helpers, someone will need to take on a facilitator role in terms of liaison and organisation. One model for self-help groups for bereaved parents is provided by The Compassionate Friends, with local co-ordinators who act as contact points.

One advantage of self-selection is the potential for minority groups to meet together, such as parents who have been bereaved of a child through suicide or murder.

Led groups

Support groups set up by professional or voluntary workers offer the security of leadership, which helps to facilitate the work of the group. The formation of the group may be in response to request or perceived need. The role of the leader(s) may be a passive one, keeping time boundaries and facilitating introductions; or it may be more directive, with structured meetings around themes or tasks. In any case the leader will act as a kind of container for the group which makes it a very stressful role. The importance of planning, clear aims, ground rules and good support/supervision for the leaders cannot be overestimated, and these issues will be addressed in Chapter 9. Obviously a therapeutic group requires skilled leadership.

The advantage of led groups for the members is that they are released from responsibility for the group and feel safer to express difficult feelings. There will also be a degree of detachment in the leader, which enables her to orchestrate the group, so that everyone who wishes to speak has an opportunity to be heard.

Structure – open or closed?

An open group is one that has a fluctuating membership, open to all-comers with a free option whether and when to attend. This flexibility is welcome to those who feel the need for support at particular times, and may not wish to attend when they are feeling specially vulnerable or when they are enjoying a 'good patch'. If there is no consistent core of members, however, it can be difficult for newcomers to build trust in the group. The fact that newcomers are joining the group all the time also means that open groups go on from week to week or month to month, without any natural end. Newer members may welcome this, reassured by the presence of bereaved people who are further on in their journey; longer-term members may eventually find it less helpful to be constantly drawn back to the early days of grieving. On the other hand, an open group has the advantage of doing away with expectations about how anyone should be or behave according to the length of their bereavement.

A closed group is one that has a selected membership over a fixed period of time, and is likely to be more structured than an open group. A fixed term group is the preferred choice of most professionals who act as facilitators for several reasons:

- it is more manageable in terms of their own commitment
- it promotes trust and continuity for the members, who are therefore able to risk more of their true feelings
- it prevents dependence
- it confronts the harsh reality of moving on.

A closed group seems more appropriate for those who share common features in their bereavement, for example a group of parents who have lost a child from the same illness in the same hospital over the same period of time. It is perhaps less appropriate for those whose loss leaves little chance of adjustment, such as parents who have lost an older child for whom they have cared over many years.

There are obvious advantages to setting limits on the life of a group, whether that marks the end of the group or provides a natural break before reconvening.

Social activities

Shared activity can be a wonderful therapy in its own right. It is particularly attractive to those who have no time for counselling or groups but who welcome the chance to mix with others who share their special experience. Social events, physical activity, fundraising organisation and committee work all provide the opportunity for oblique support. Purposeful activity seems to be a natural coping mechanism for many men who are distrustful of emotion or see themselves in the stronger supportive role in the family.

Children are usually better disposed towards doing things than talking about feelings they are unsure about. In the early 1990s, Alder Centre expeditions to Northumberland to swim with Freddie the dolphin proved enormously popular and provided the opportunity for bereaved siblings to share experiences that had marked them out in another way. Planning and preparation brought them together socially, and the encounters with Freddie gave them a sense of being special as well as different. For one of those youngsters, the adventure also gave her the confidence to talk about the death of her sister for the first time. Their families came together to watch video recordings and share photographs.

As well as reducing isolation, social activities for adults can be fun too! Quiz nights, country walks and shared holidays bring people together to enjoy the good things of life. These are not only welcome diversions but also affirmations of one's place in the world and the right to take pleasure in it alongside the pain of grief. This was the comment of one mother after a week spent in the Lake District with other parents:

'I now know the meaning of holidays and what they are for, which since the death of my child I had forgotten.'

Shared family holidays can provide the opportunity to enjoy again an activity which may have lost its meaning.

Support for children

Various references have been made to the difficulties surrounding children's support needs. Parents who are overwhelmed by their own grief may find it hard to attend to the needs of their surviving children. Adults struggle to gain access to the understanding and feelings of children who have not developed the emotional language to express themselves. Children seek to protect their carers from distress as much as their carers try to shield them from the painful reality of death. As a result, children often become 'the forgotten mourners' when a sibling or friend dies. For those helpers who are aware of children's needs, the question remains of how to provide for them – particularly when dealing with very young children – which will avoid problems later on.

The most important factor which determines how children cope with loss is the attitude of the parents. Young children suffer most the *secondary* losses, such as lack of attention and the loss of security in an ordered world, when a sibling dies. If the parents are able to include their other children in their experience of loss, keeping them involved and informed, while at the same time maintaining a sense of safety and security in the family, then they will cope well. Parents are best placed to answer a child's questions and provide reassurance to counter their fears and concerns.

It follows, then, that the best way of supporting children is through the parents. First of all that means providing adequate support for the parents. Second, parents can be briefed as to how best to support their other children at the time of the bereavement. Remind parents that children will 'read' the emotions around them and overhear conversations, and will ask questions either directly or indirectly. The Foundation for the Study of Infant Deaths and cot death associations have highlighted the needs of siblings, publishing leaflets and training befrienders to raise the issues with parents. The Compassionate Friends also publish helpful articles on the grief of sibling children and teenagers and how to help them to understand death.

Advice to parents for the benefit of children

- If at all possible, keep the family together.
- Keep children informed about what is happening. Even very young children will sense distress and need to know its cause. It is

better for children to hear unpleasant things from their parents than from strangers.

- Answer children's questions as honestly as you can.
- Reassure them that the death of their brother or sister was not their fault or responsibility.
- Do not be afraid of using the word 'death'. Children get confused and worried by phrases like 'gone to sleep' or 'taken by Jesus'. Avoid fairy tales to explain death, and do not be afraid to admit that you do not know all the answers. The more openly your family can talk about death, the easier it is for the child to accept it.
- Allow your children to feel sad, angry and all the natural feelings of grief, although do not expect them to feel sad all the time.
- When young children include some aspect of the death in their play, this is normal and healthy. The same goes for telling strangers 'My little brother is dead'.
- Do not be afraid to show your own grief in front of your children. This will help them to grieve, and reassure them that you loved the child who died.
- Give constant reassurance that you love and care equally for these children too. Give them special times, and listen.
- Do ask for help if you feel unable to deal with your children during this time.

If parents are not able to be the primary carers for a while, or are emotionally incapable of giving this kind of attention, then many of the above tasks can be undertaken by a relative. The family may enrol the help of a member of the clergy, a teacher, a social worker or a health visitor to talk to a child or answer her questions. This should always be done in consultation with the parents, and if possible in their presence.

How far should a professional take the initiative in cases where the parents seem unaware of their child's needs? Such situations require great sensitivity in explaining to parents the cause for concern and gaining their co-operation. Working with the parents to win their trust brings the best chance of success.

In any case, talking to a child about death and allowing the expression of bereft feelings cannot be done in a vacuum. It needs to be done within the context of a trusting and caring relationship, with time for the child to talk and react.

See Chapter 6 for further guidance on talking with children and for information on behavioural reactions.

Innovative groupwork and projects for children

It has long been recognised that bereaved children have special needs, and that most children benefit from meeting with other bereaved siblings. This recognition has resulted in the development of groups for children where their needs can be addressed in the supportive setting of being with others who have had similar experiences. For some children this is therapeutic in itself. At the beginning of a group for bereaved siblings when group members were introducing themselves, I remember the relief shown on the face of a boy of 12 when he realised that another group member had also lost *two* siblings, as he had, and he no longer felt a freak.

After the reassurance of shared experience, the group offers ways of revisiting grief issues, understanding their losses and celebrating memories, of discovering ways of relating and having fun. Northamptonshire Social Services have developed a group work approach which has been echoed in many other parts of the country, offering youngsters the opportunity to socialise, work together and play together within a structure of activities planned by concerned and committed professionals. They certainly need to be committed, as this work is demanding and time consuming in terms of the preparations, practicalities, skills and emotional resources. Typically, the group will meet for eight to 10 weekly sessions with a structured programme which can be made flexible to the members' needs.

The work of the Stockport Children's Bereavement *Kingfisher* Project has focused on running such groups. In the 1990s, a multi-disciplinary team was made up of professionals from a variety of backgrounds – child psychology, Macmillan nursing, social work, health visiting – who contributed group work skills and their different experiences of working with children. Referrals came from health, education and social services, regarding children and young people whose difficult bereavements had led to concerns about their moods and behaviour. Each child and family was assessed before inviting the child to join an age-appropriate group, and the parents/carers to join a support group running at the same time as the children's group. Weekly group supervision of all the group leaders monitored the development of the groups as well as providing support for such emotionally demanding work. Evaluation of the groups brought overwhelmingly positive reporting of the benefits gained by individual children and their families.

As happens all too often with such projects, uncertain funding has halted the development of the Stockport Project for the time being, risking the loss of the significant learning and expertise built up over several years. Hopefully, this will prove to be a temporary pause.

Liverpool Children's Project, funded by The Children's Society, followed a similar path of development, though working within more flexible frameworks. The age range of the children in any one group was wider, the membership more variable, and the length of the group more open-ended. The content focused more on social activities and being with other children, rather than activities directly addressing loss experiences.

Also in Liverpool, the Alder Centre has established two-day residential therapeutic breaks for bereaved siblings. These breaks are facilitated by counsellors at the Centre together with professionals from within the Hospital Trust (play worker, social worker, psychologist etc). Each group has a maximum of 12 members aged between five and 12, who have been bereaved for six months or more. A variation of this pattern is for the group to meet for five weekly sessions and then to spend a day together, with family involvement in the first and last sessions.

Most people have heard of the Winston's Wish Project in Gloucestershire which has led the field in this pioneering work with children. A range of services now includes individual work and social activities for children, advice and information for parents and support for schools, as well as the Camp Winston residential weekends for children and similar weekends for parents which have featured on television documentaries. Although the Project can only deal with referrals within the county of Gloucestershire, Winston's Wish has inspired the development of grief support programmes all over the UK, and the Project offers help to others through training and consultancy work. The Project's leaflet includes these words:

> 'At Winston's Wish we believe all our services should be routinely available to every family. Most families need straightforward support, *not therapy*. It is our aim to ensure that all bereaved families can have the services they need when they feel the time is right.'

Throughout their work the emphasis is on supporting the child within and through the family system. Specifically, their aims include the encouragement of open communication in families and helping families to find ways of remembering the person who has died.

All the projects mentioned above in some way involve the child's parents. This is a welcome move forward from services which aim to support children in isolation from their parents and families. Such a separation is not only a false one, but it compounds any feelings of isolation which the child may already have experienced during and after the death of her sibling. These are the comments of one bereaved parent, based on the experience of her own surviving child and observations of the experience of siblings in other families:

> 'The trouble is – and I know the lack of resources is a problem – child loss is often dealt with as separate issues for parents and siblings, without realising that the two cannot be separated. Dealing with siblings in isolation replicates what happens at home, i.e. they are often excluded and isolated by their parents,

and counsellors who work with bereaved parents may sometimes miss the effects on remaining children and family
dynamics. Losing a child affects every family member differently,
which in itself alters family structures.'

References

Green J (1991) Death with dignity: meeting the spiritual needs of patients
in a multi-cultural society. *Nursing Times.*

Herbert M (1996) *Supporting Bereaved and Dying Children and Their
Parents.* The British Psychological Society, Leicester.

Hill L (ed) (1994) *Caring for Dying Children and Their Families.* Chapman
& Hall, London.

Lendrum S and Syme G (1992) *Gift of Tears.* Routledge, London.

Neuberger J (1987) *Caring for Dying People of Different Faiths.* Austen
Cornish, London.

8 Support for schools

'Grief should be the instructor of the wise;
sorrow is knowledge.'

Byron

How schools are affected

After the family, the school community contains the people most affected by the death of a child – friends, playmates, fellow students, teachers, auxiliary staff. Parents and governors form part of the wider school community. Whether the death is anticipated or sudden, it may well be the first bereavement experience for the child's peers and for younger teachers too. Close attachments are formed between children and their teachers, particularly in the infant and junior school, so that the death of a child may be a personal as well as professional loss. Teachers have a highly developed sense of responsibility, and if the death occurs when they are in charge, they will be vulnerable to extreme stress. Dealing with death is not easy for teachers who are confined by a culture of being in control and having answers. When dealing with their own emotions, they rarely have their own space to retreat to, and are constantly paying attention to the demands of large numbers of children throughout the school day.

For the pupils, the closer they were to the child and the circumstances of the death, the more profound will be the consequences in terms of self-esteem, concentration and attainment levels. Follow-up studies on survivors of the *Jupiter* cruise ship sinking in 1988 showed significant effects on academic performance, after comparing end of year exam results before and after the incident for survivors and for non-cruise students (Dagwell, Tsui and Yule, 1993).

Two longer-term studies on the effects of the sinking of the *Jupiter* by Yule *et al.* have been published in the *Journal of Child Psychology and Psychiatry*. They show that following the accident, 52% of the affected teenagers developed symptoms of post-traumatic stress disorder, mostly within the first weeks. 15% still experienced these symptoms 5–7 years later. Overall, there was a three-fold increase in mental health problems, and the survivors developed depression and anxiety disorders to a far greater extent than control groups. Thus, what seemed to some like a frightening but minor disaster has been shown to have had major consequences.

The impact on the school as an organisation is often under-estimated by outsiders, sometimes even by school managers them-selves. Tragedy and trauma carry the potential both for bringing out the best in people, and for magnifying any underlying difficulties. Most deaths of school-age children will be as the result of critical incidents, so it is worth looking at what happens to organisations under stress. The model pictured in Figure 8.1 is derived from the work of Carolyn Attneave (1973) in helping to deal with community crises in Canada over a 20-year period. Observed phases help to

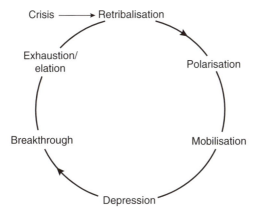

Figure 8.1 Response to crisis model (Attneave and Speck, 1973).

understand and predict ways in which the school is likely to respond to crisis:

1 *Retribalisation*

This word describes the initial process of the community closing ranks, huddling together, wanting to keep out strangers etc. It is seen as a healthy early response to crisis and should be respected by outsiders seeking to help.

2 *Polarisation*

A polarising of attitudes commonly occurs, for example between those who want to stop all normal activities and those who want to carry on as though nothing has happened. Healthy organisations can acknowledge and discuss these differences to prevent any destructive splitting. Help may be needed from outside to facilitate this.

3 *Mobilisation*

If phase 2 has been negotiated, now people can begin positive action. Comfort is offered, connections made, feelings of loss and guilt are shared. Support from outside should concentrate on facilitating what others can do for themselves.

4 *Depression*

This is the inevitable realisation that nothing will be the same again. A sense of despair spreads through the system as the absolute nature of the loss sinks in. The maintenance of support systems and monitoring of different needs are important.

5 *Breakthrough*

Realisation of survival releases the potential to help others, while those who continue to feel helpless will remain in the depression phase. There may be a role for outside support to help different groups recognise their different stages and needs.

6 *Exhaustion/elation*

Lack of sleep, exercise etc will catch up with people at this point and rest becomes necessary. Someone apart from the centre of things may need to say 'Go home now, you've done enough'. Another feature of this phase may be pride and pleasure in having come through the crisis, and outsiders can help by recognising people's courage and coping.

Inner resources and outside help

Attneave's model gives some pointers as to when support from outside the immediate school community might be appropriate. Schools are well used to dealing with crises, know their own systems, and develop their own coping strategies. The imposition of unbidden help from outside, however well meaning, will be counter product-ive, as the result will be to disempower the school from using its natural resources. Also, strangers who come in to the school to talk to children about (the) death deny them the benefit of familiar and trusted adults to help restore their sense of security.

The experience of a Kidderminister school, after 12 of its children and a teacher were killed on the M40 in 1993, provided salutary lessons. Three teams of counsellors had arrived at the school on the first chaotic day after the accident, all of them unknown to the school – this simply added to the chaos. This experience highlighted the need for co-ordinated responses which first of all respect the school's natural resources – which in this case were rooted in the culture of the Roman Catholic church. The familiar local priest and parish helpers provided more effective support for this school than the teams of external counsellors.

The most efficient bereavement support systems are aptly illus-trated in Figure 8.2. O'Hara (1996) reminds us that those nearest to the child provide the most natural support. The 'specialists' from outside the community are better placed for supporting those who support the children, notably the teachers.

Obviously, children need the love and comfort of parents and family when a child dies. The next most important adults are their teachers, who have a vital part to play as role models as well as edu-cators. Usually they know instinctively what is best for the children, and will only need some reassurance that they can allow them-selves to be open, honest and distressed in front of the children.

Figure 8.2 Bereavement support systems (© O'Hara M [Salford EPS] 1996).

When children are trusted with such openness they often surprise their teachers with their acceptance, generosity, imagination and resilience.

Planning and preparation

It is no surprise that schools deal better with a pupil's death if they are prepared. Although every situation is unique, and nothing can prevent feelings of shock and helplessness when the death occurs, there are common features which can be anticipated. Whether the death is expected or sudden, outcomes relate to three key areas: *communication, curriculum,* and *contingency plans.*

When the death is expected

Fortunately death from chronic illness such as childhood leukaemia or congenital disorder is now a comparatively rare event. Usually the family and school will keep in close contact as the disease progresses, and the class teacher is often the key link person. Communication is all-important, between family and school, between teachers and children. Conveying the seriousness of the situation as the child nears death, without conveying loss of hope, is a tricky task. However, preparation in some form facilitates the giving of the news when the child dies. Time and thought can be given beforehand as to how the children will be told, who attends the funeral, how feelings can be expressed and memories ritualised.

Good communication will depend partly on open and trusting relationships, and partly on how life and death issues are dealt with as part of the curriculum. As a generalisation it is probably true that there is now less of a taboo over discussing death with children, though how possible it is for children to explore death and dying will depend largely on how far teachers have tackled their own anxieties on the subject. In some schools 'death studies' are included in the PSHE curriculum, while related areas of study (including religious studies, biology, nature studies, and health and social care) all offer opportunities for developing understanding and vocabulary around death. Certainly it must help to deal with the death of a child if the school already has a language to speak in and reference points to use. (*See also* Chapter 6 on guidelines for talking with children.)

When the death is sudden

The death may be unexpected, as in the case of meningitis or an undiagnosed heart condition, or it may be as the result of a traumatic event – accident, murder, suicide, atrocity, disaster. It seems that man-made disasters such as Hillsborough, Hungerford and Dunblane are harder to come to terms with than natural disasters such as the Towyn floods. Again, public disasters carry more potential for shared experience and professional help, whereas private tragedies are more isolating and harder to deal with. There is plenty of research and literature now available to endorse the value of being as prepared as possible for the unexpected tragedy or critical incident. In 1993 all schools in the UK were issued with a free copy of *Wise Before the*

Event, by William Yule and Anne Gold, funded by the Gulbenkian Foundation. This booklet spelt out clearly the case for making contingency plans which will lessen the impact on the school when a crisis occurs. Having argued the case for planning, to reduce the impact of physical and emotional effects of disaster, the authors offered strategies for schools to adapt and adopt as their own contingency plans. These guidelines have inspired many LEA initiatives to develop frameworks for the management and support of critical incidents and to encourage individual schools to set up their own protocols.

The work of Afra Ayalon in Israel, Atle Dyregrov in Norway, and Elizabeth Capewell in the UK in the 1990s has encouraged the shift from schools reacting to a crisis, to a prepared and proactive range of interventions. Otherwise the same principles apply as to expected deaths: children and their teachers benefit from good communication and awareness of death issues via the curriculum.

Specifically, what can schools do to prepare?

This process has been followed by some schools in recent years:

- set up a group of staff/governors to research the available literature, local guidelines and recent experience
- formulate an action plan (*see* below)
- establish a critical incident management team and identify key roles
- ensure that basic information, contact lists, communication systems and emergency procedures are in place and regularly updated
- carry out a simulation exercise to test out how a critical incident might unfold
- familiarise all staff and governors with action plans and procedures
- review the adequacy of curriculum coverage of death and loss issues
- identify training needs for staff.

The LEA has a crucially important role in supporting this process and responding to identified training needs. The Local Education Officer and other identified personnel should be on hand to offer practical support, and will probably act as key communication points within the school's action plan.

Trauma-related deaths of children will involve the emergency services, and the police will take control of certain procedures.

Action plans for managing critical incidents

As an example, Cheshire LEA recommends the following action plan to its schools as a structure which can be readily adapted to most situations. Other LEAs offer similar models, based on the *Wise Before the Event* booklet. This plan assumes that the school has a critical incident management team with identified roles. *Within hours:*

- gather information about what has happened
- brief the critical incident management team, and allocate responsible adults to places where they are needed, e.g. hospital, child's home, administrative support
- use LEA support network through designated contacts
- allocate space as an incident management room with an exclusive phone line or use of a mobile phone
- contact families whose children are involved, and make arrangements for informing other parents
- inform teaching and support staff
- inform the pupils
- be ready to deal with the media.

As soon as possible:

- prepare strategies for handling the reactions of people affected (*see* below)
- anticipate further information bulletins for parents not directly involved

- anticipate further media interest; liaise with the LEA press officer or public relations department.

These pointers can act as a very useful checklist at a time when shock, panic and feelings of helplessness can threaten to overwhelm the most competent of school managers.

A question which is often faced in the immediate aftermath of a traumatic death is *'should the school be closed?'* There may, of course, be practical and safety factors to take into account. Psychologically, it is likely to be a mistake to assume that people – children or staff – are better off at home. Excepting the case of a school-based atrocity such as Dunblane, people need to be with others similarly affected after traumatic events to share their reactions, and people need the security of familiar faces, places and routines to help them through the dislocation of the first days. The school is also a natural community meeting place for parents, many of whom will be drawn to the school for information and reassurance. Schools often find themselves unprepared for this, and surprised that the bereaved parents usually want to visit the school soon after the death. Anecdotally, this happened in one primary school the same day that the child died, much to the con-sternation of the headteacher, who felt inadequate to face dis-traught and possibly angry parents. In the event, the parents simply wanted to be where their child should have been that day, and to make contact with the other adults who had been such an integral part of their child's life. The headteacher and classteacher felt as comforted by the parents as the other way round.

Psychological support: who does what and when?

Two important guiding principles have already been established.

1 Schools cope better with the death of a pupil when they have established systems of communication. This applies to the ethos of the school, and its ability to talk about emotional needs, as well as to protocols for conveying information.
2 A school's natural support resources need to be respected, especially with regard to the emotional needs of grieving children.

Having said that, there is a time and place for external supports. First, school staff who are providing support for children in their roles as closest trusted adults, will themselves need support. The concept of Winnicott's 'nursing triad' applies here, in that the primary carer needs to be 'held' to sustain the role, particularly when that caring role involves the containment of negative emotions. Second, staff have their own grief to deal with, which may expose them to other personal griefs and anxieties, and some may feel the need for more support than can be offered by colleagues. Third, there will be incidents involving the death of a child when teachers and other school staff are so directly involved in the trauma as to be incapacitated themselves, either physically or emotionally.

The catch-all term for any kind of emotional or psychological support is '*counselling*', as in media accounts which report that 'counselling will be available to the survivors' and 'counsellors are at hand at the site of the incident'. Local and national government members may also seek reassurance from school managers that *counsellors* are involved, as demonstrating that all is being done that is possible, and that specialist help is being provided. The reality is that counselling is a specific kind of support which is not appropriate to the immediate situation. An analogy from the medical world might be to send for a physiotherapist when first aid is required! Sadly, some families after Lockerbie and Dunblane experienced inappropriate, untimely 'counselling' as intrusive (BBC, 1996).

Another expectation which has developed after major incidents is that a telephone helpline should be set up. Yvonne McEwan, director of the Department of Trauma Management at Abertay Fife University Centre, is one of those who questions the value of a helpline which may actually foster helplessness and anxiety in callers (BBC, 1996). Unless the helpline has a clearly defined remit, such as the provision of practical information following a meningitis outbreak, it may well prove to be a knee-jerk reaction to feelings of helplessness in those who want to help, or want to be seen as helping.

In order to clarify what kinds of psychological help are appropriate at different times, it will be useful first to consider the needs commonly experienced in reaction to the traumatic death of a child in a school community, and then to relate these needs to different levels of support.

Common reactions

Obviously reactions will vary according to the grieving individual's age and experience, the nature of the death and other circumstances, though it is possible to anticipate common emotional reactions. Not surprisingly, the most common reactions include *denial, distress, guilt, anger, helplessness.*

For those closely affected by a critical incident fatality, common reactions will include some of the classic post-traumatic stress symptoms associated with increased levels of arousal, re-experiencing the event, and avoidance of trigger stimuli. These can be simply understood as the stressful tension between the need to remember what has happened – in order to believe it and make sense of it – and the need to forget what has happened, because it is too painful or overwhelming. Normal reactions to these abnormal events commonly include *hyper-anxiety, irritability, sleep disturbance, flashbacks, detachment, lack of concentration, survivor guilt.*

The impact of a traumatic death on the school as an organisation can also be predicted (*see* pp 181–2). Existing strengths and vulnerabilities are likely to be magnified, and polarities may develop between different parts of the school community as it struggles to come to terms with what has happened.

Common needs

It follows from the above that common needs can be anticipated, and certain actions taken, to provide the best conditions for the school's recovery and to look after the mental health of its pupils and staff.

- Prompt, accurate and regular information about the incident is top priority. Anxiety and anger are fuelled by uncertainty and delay.
- As soon as possible, the school management needs to acknowledge what has happened and the sadness or horror of it, perhaps via year assemblies, class announcements, letters home.
- Staff and children need the opportunity to talk about what has happened, to ask questions, and to express their personal reactions. This is most naturally done in familiar small groups, though it may also be appropriate to set aside a dedicated space in school where people can come and talk together about the dead child(ren) and find ways to express their thoughts and feelings in writing and drawing. Extra staff meetings give the opportunity to process reactions, monitor developments and work through different perspectives.
- There is a need for the school to connect with the dead child's family and wider community through informal contacts and formal rituals. Families usually welcome the active participation of the school in the funeral arrangements, and their own involvement in school memorial services. In the longer term, anniversaries should be planned for and handled with sensitivity.
- When something dreadful has happened, there is a need for the security of familiar faces and surroundings and normal routines. Alongside the recognitions and rituals, the continuity of the school day and regular activities provide some measure of reassurance in a world suddenly made unsafe and unpredictable. Where staff are incapacitated, governors and parents can prove invaluable classroom assistants.

- Those providing front-line support, including administrative and auxiliary staff, need their own support. Relief cover should be anticipated for key staff who face additional stresses such as dealing with the media or anxious visitors. Senior managers, who usually cope very well with the immediate crisis, should be prepared for the time when their personal reactions catch up and need attention.
- Teachers and children who survived the fatal incident will need special support on their return to school. Discussion and planning will aid reintegration.

Siblings have their own special needs and present particular challenges to the school. Older children should be consulted as to how their peers and teachers can best help, and younger children given opportunities to express their feelings through drawing and play.

> 'Schools represent continuity for children in times of crisis. When a traumatic event directly strikes a school, it is important that the school continues as a supportive and stable part of the students' environment.'
>
> Dyregrov, 1993

Levels of support

The following levels of support are suggested as offering another way of looking at who does what and when.

Level 1: 'Someone there'

At the time of the fatal incident or in the immediate aftermath, the obvious priority is the comforting presence of another human being to offer practical support. This may be given by literally offering a helping hand, a shoulder to cry on, a blanket, a hot drink, a mobile phone. Such support is typically provided by emergency services, neighbours, colleagues, and – in a large scale disaster – voluntary agencies such as the WRVS and Salvation Army.

Level 2: 'A listening ear'

Immediately or soon after the event there is the need for most people to talk – about what has just happened, about their immediate concerns. What is required at this stage may include reassurance, information or advice, but is essentially the ability to listen, accept and understand – basic listening skills. It may be provided by emergency services (if they have the time), colleagues, managers, school governors, statutory and voluntary services. This process of rehearsing the events and of discharging one's immediate reactions is sometimes called 'defusing'.

Level 3: 'Debriefing'

Not to be confused with defusing, this word describes a structured opportunity to talk through reactions to the incident and death, following a formula which seeks to integrate the experience and normalise the reactions. This support strategy belongs to the short term, between a few days and a few weeks after the event, and certainly after the first numbing effects and shock have subsided. Debriefing may take place one-to-one or more usually in a group with others similarly affected. It is believed to reduce the likelihood of long-term stress (post traumatic stress disorder), though research findings are so far limited and inconclusive. The techniques involved have been adapted from those used with combat and war survivors, and their application require skills training, sensitivity and a structured support system for those delivering the service.

Atle Dyregrov, a Norwegian educationalist, has developed debriefing techniques with particular application to schools. Debriefing may be provided by any of the professional/statutory services personnel who have been prepared and trained. In recent years some LEAs have developed special critical incident response teams who have been trained in debriefing methods. Educational psychology, learning support and advisory services are obvious resources for members of such teams.

Level 4: 'Counselling sessions'

Longer term counselling, for those whose stress reactions persist and cause difficulties which hinder the return to normal functioning, offers the opportunity to work through their issues and learn new coping strategies. Individually contracted sessions will be tailor-made and provided by people who are properly trained and qualified to maintain a professional counselling relationship. One of the criteria to satisfy these conditions will be that the counsellor has received professional counselling training apart from their skills training as a teacher, nurse etc. Another is the provision of counselling supervision, and the counsellor must be a member of a relevant professional body. Occupational health departments usually provide counselling services for staff.

Level 5: 'Specialist referral'

This need will be indicated by severe and persistent PTSD symptoms which prevent any kind of normal functioning. Referrals would normally be via the medical route to psychological or psychiatric services. In some parts of the country there are centres and clinics which specialise in PTSD work. Intensive therapy may be behavioural, cognitive or relate to other difficult life experiences which have been reactivated. Suitable providers of these services obviously need to have the specialist training, qualifications and supervision to equip them adequately for this work.

Advice and guidance

The school will benefit from having access to advice and guidance throughout their experience of the death of a pupil. There is an ongoing process of monitoring reactions and assessing support needs, and even the most self-sufficient school community will usefully refer to outside resources for reassurance and support.

At a stressful time, school managers are likely to turn to someone who is already known to the school, so it may be worth the effort to make contact with any specialist resources for advice and guidance *before* they are needed. They may have useful information to offer on how other schools have managed similar situations; on which children will be particularly vulnerable; on useful reading materials and references. Does the LEA have an adviser with responsibility for such advice and guidance? For independent and private schools, is there access to an external consultant?

In certain situations and at certain times, consultation will appropriately lead to the direct intervention of external support; but for the most part the consultant's job is to empower teachers and school managers in using their own skills and resources.

What of those schools whose managers adopt the 'stiff upper lip' to emotional distress and deny the impact on the school, themselves or others? There is no doubt that the headteacher's attitude is a crucial factor, and s/he acts as a role model for staff and children. Senior managers promote the ethos of the school and its value system. It is their responsibility to assess the needs of staff and pupils in the light of what is now known about the impact of the life-threatening events and sudden death. In this task they are accountable to parents, governors and to the wider community.

If the school is intolerant of emotional need, the following myths may operate:

- *'Infants don't understand about death, are not affected, don't need to be told.'*
- *'The child who died didn't go to our school, so there's no need to mention it.'*
- *'The children will lose confidence in their teachers if they see them upset.'*
- *'We have a wonderful pastoral system, so we don't need any help.'*
- *'The children don't seem to be upset, so they must be all right.'*
- *'Encouraging the expression of feelings will lead to mass hysteria.'*

Challenging such myths needs to take place *before* the death of a child, at a time when these defences are not so strong. Assessment and review of the school's contingency plans and curriculum provision are good places to start. These processes can be initiated by anyone from a range of interested people, including staff, parents, governors, advisers and inspectors.

Summary of key points

- Don't underestimate the impact of a child's death on the school.
- Healing comes from within, supported by outsiders.
- Planning and preparation pay dividends.
- Reactions and support needs can be anticipated, and then matched with appropriate resources.
- Information and communication are paramount.
- People need permission to talk and cry.
- Rituals and normality restore security.

References

Ayalon O and Flasher A (1993) *Chain Reaction.* Jessica Kingsley, London.

Capewell E (1993) Critical incident management in schools: headteachers' briefing. *Croner.* **28**: 4–5 and **29**: 5–7.

Capewell E (1994) Responding to children in trauma: a systems approach for schools. *Bereavement Care.* **Spring**: 2–7.

Cheshire County Council (1999) *Managing the Response to Critical Incidents in Schools.* CCC, Chester.

Dagwell K, Tsui E and Yule W (1993) *Effects of a Disaster on Children's Attainment.* Unpublished.

Dyregrov A (1994) *Grief in Children.* Jessica Kingsley, London.

Gold A and Yule W (1993) *Wise Before The Event.* Calouste Gulbenkian Foundation.

McEwan Y (1997) A challenge to the counselling culture. *Nursing Standard.* **12**(2).

O'Hara DM, Taylor R and Simpson K (1994) Critical incident stress debriefing: bereavement support in schools. Developing a role for an LEA educational psychology service. *Educational Psychology in Practice.* **10**(1): 27–34.

Winnicott D (1971) *Playing and Reality.* Tavistock, London.

9 Support services

'The death of a child is not something to be joked about, or laughed at. It is an event from which a parent does not recover: life is never quite the same again, nor should be, for now it incorporates an unnatural event. We do not expect to outlive our children, nor do we want to. On the other hand, life must go on, if only for the sake of those who are left, and, what is more, it is our duty to learn to enjoy it again. For what do we regret for those untimely dead, but the opportunity to live with enjoyment? If we are to give proper meaning and honour to their death, and our grief, we must enjoy the life we, and not they, are privileged to have, and live thereafter properly and well, without wranglings or rancour.'

Fay Weldon, *The Hearts and Lives of Men*

As the special needs of bereaved families and communities become better recognised, various initiatives are developed to provide support. Some thrive while others prove short-lived, and the difference between the two is often put down to chance. It will be proposed here that the success of any support service will depend first on meeting certain core conditions, and second on good planning and preparation. These will be applied to the setting up of a support group, but could equally well be applied to starting a helpline or befriending service. Finally, the way forward to improve bereavement care will focus on the need for co-ordinated services, better information and pro-active support.

Core conditions

Some basic principles apply to the establishment of any support service, whether it be a group, befriending, counselling or a multi-purpose centre.

Identifying the need

This means consulting those who are perceived as needing support at the time. One difficulty is that people do not always know what they want in their distress, or whether the support being offered will suit them. In this case the helper can draw on the past experience of families and consult other professionals. Another possible factor is that well-meaning carers may be more concerned about 'doing something to help' than responding to actual need. Indeed, an assessment of support needs may indicate a separate agenda for the professional or volunteer, which will have to be recognised and accommodated. Assessment also involves identifying existing means of support, to ensure that services are not duplicated.

Sufficiency of resources

Too often, bereavement support initiatives fizzle out for want of adequate resources. Perhaps after a first flush of enthusiasm, just a few volunteers are left to cope with too many demands. Sometimes an initiative will depend on the commitment of one dedicated individual, whose bereavement work is not recognised as part of the job: when that person moves on, the project collapses. Sufficiency of resources relates to people, time, space and money. Although the setting up of any new service requires an act of faith, it is irresponsible to do so without reasonable confidence that the service can be sustained over a period of time, especially when working with loss and grief.

Support systems

Care for the carers is essential in such an emotionally demanding area of work. Management and administrative structures are necessary to any support system, however informal.

Key questions need to be addressed at the research and planning stage relating to the type and scope of the proposed service.

- At whom is the service aimed?
- What does the service aim to achieve?
- What are the geographical boundaries?
- What is already being done?
- What is the preferred setting?
- Who will deliver the service?
- What are the criteria for taking referrals?
- Who will manage and supervise the work?

At all stages it is important to work co-operatively with those with common interests and seek their support. Bereavement projects, by nature of the subject, tend to attract defensive attitudes! Canvassing for a broad base of support also ensures that your plans are in line with progressive thinking and good practice in other areas.

Starting a support group

The guidelines suggested here assume that professional or voluntary workers are responding to perceived needs of bereaved family members, which may be met by offering a group experience. For the sake of convenience I shall refer to the potential group participants as parents, although of course they may be grandparents or siblings. The process will be the same, except that a sibling group will need parental agreement, and its leaders will require some understanding of children's perceptions.

Identifying the need

The impetus to start a group tends to fall into one of three categories.

1 In response to requests from parents to meet other parents for mutual support.
2 In anticipation of griefwork which can be facilitated in a thera-peutic setting.
3 As an economical way of coping with limited resources to offer individual help.

Being clear about the purpose will affect the direction you take and determine the appropriate type of group (*see* Chapter 7 for an out-line of different group types). Whatever the impetus, it is important not to be pressured into starting a group before adequate preparation. This may be frustrating for potential participants, who will welcome regular communication during the planning stages.

The consultation process includes an audit of what is happening elsewhere to avoid duplicating resources, and making links with other colleagues, agencies and disciplines to ensure a broad base of support for the venture. Management may require data to back up any application for time or other resources and to clarify issues such as confidentiality.

Calling a meeting

An open meeting of all interested parties needs a clear agenda, some-one to take a chairing role and someone to take names and notes. If likely attenders of the group are not present, their views should be represented.

The primary purpose of this first meeting is to take an audit of concerns, current practice, interests and resources.

- It is helpful to begin with introductions by name, role, agency representation and reason for attending. Some may see this initiative as a means of getting recognition for the work they already do for bereaved families or to gain understanding of their own support needs: it is important that these concerns are acknowledged by the Chair so that they can be openly identified and separated from the parents' needs.

- The purpose of the group, in the kind of general terms that can be summarised in one sentence, should then be agreed.
- The type and status of group required can then be discussed, along with the implications for resources. It may not be possible to reach a consensus at this stage.
- Another audit follows of the kind of help and commitment attenders are willing and able to give.
- A *small* working party can now take the findings forward to the next planning stage. There tends to be a high level of enthusiasm at this first meeting, so beware the 'hands up to volunteer' approach! Some means of communicating progress needs to be agreed, and dates set if the working party is to report back to another general meeting.

Planning

The planning tasks cover objectives, method, structure and programme, and a number of meetings may be needed.

- *Objectives*: these spell out the aim and purpose in specific terms. What will the group need to achieve its purpose? What conditions need to be met?
- *Method*: what kind of group (open or closed, self-help or led, spontaneous or planned) will be most appropriate? What size, composition and setting will help to meet the objectives?
- *Structure*: this provides boundaries for the group and moves on to practicalities. These will include:
  - setting dates for starting (and finishing)
  - deciding the venue
  - agreeing the personnel to facilitate the group

- guidelines for access, referral and selection
- publicity
- arranging support and supervision for leaders
- setting dates for evaluation.
- *Programme*: the facilitators/leaders of the group will need to be involved, if not already part of the working party, to plan timing, format and – if appropriate – the content of group meetings. If canvassing for participants, a rough guide to uptake is that one in three will respond. Parents who wish to attend the group should be visited beforehand if possible.

Delivery

Thought needs to be given to the preparation of the room, who will welcome the group members, how the group will start and how it will end. Finishing group meetings can be very difficult, but it is important to draw the session to a close, gently but firmly, at the time stated. Groups that go on till midnight are exhausting for all concerned. Parents who are overwhelmed by exposure to never-ending pain are likely to drop out. It helps if the facilitator signals the end of the session some minutes beforehand, and at the finish time physically leaves the room or puts the kettle on.

It is essential for those in charge of the meeting, whether called hosts, leaders or facilitators, to debrief their feelings and reactions before going home and ensure that time for this is built in.

Evaluation

Groups do not always turn out as expected, even after meticulous planning! Evaluation is part of the group process, and may lead to amendments as the group goes on. At another level, the facilitators' supervisor will help them to evaluate their contribution, celebrating achievements as well as learning from mistakes. Managers and funding bodies may also require evaluative reports. When the group is time-limited, evaluation may lead to the implementation of necessary changes if another group is proposed. Open-ended groups benefit from a break of some kind, perhaps over the summer, which provides a natural time for taking stock.

A co-ordinated approach

A co-ordinated approach may be understood as one which incorporates the provision of different services, or as one which enables different service providers to work co-operatively.

Various attempts have been made to provide a range of support services under one umbrella which are flexible to different needs. The Alder Centre in Liverpool modelled one such approach, followed by the Laura Centre in Leicester and the Sunrise Centre in Birmingham, with remits *to support* **anyone** *affected by the death of a child*. Thus, the Alder Centre caters for group as well as individual support, for befriending as well as counselling. It accommodates the needs of bereaved parents to keep in touch through a newsletter as well as a physical place where they can be with the memory of their dead children in a special way. Residential therapeutic breaks are organised for families and for siblings.

The Centre also provides a resource for both the training and support needs of professionals who work with bereaved families. For example, regular contributions are made to medical student training programmes at the Alder Hey NHS Trust, and Family Liaison police officers who deal with road fatalities, to help them develop the sensitivity and skills needed to work with families following the death of a child.

The role of bereaved parents has been instrumental to the development of the Alder Centre from its inception in 1989. Initially, they guided policy and practice to make the services relevant to their needs. While professional staff offered detachment, particular skills and expertise, the voluntary involvement of parents provided authenticity. Parent participation was experienced as therapeutic, whether as conference speaker or tea-maker. Helping others gave more purpose to the lives they were rebuilding.

'Dot is one of the parents who worked tirelessly for the Centre from the planning stage in a number of different roles at various times. As her 13-year-old daughter was approaching death, Dot asked Christine, "What do you want me to do?". Christine's answer was, "Help someone else." In the voluntary tasks she has undertaken – answering the helpline, befriending, fund-raising, talking to visitors – Dot felt that Christine was working alongside her.

Jo, Eunice and Bernie are typical of volunteer parents whose work at the Centre has fed into their own personal growth and career development. All three have become qualified counsellors. Since her son Liam's death, Bernie has also graduated in Childhood Studies which included a dissertation on sibling grief for which she gained an 80% rating. "I was really thrilled to get this result but also sad because the subject matter depended on the fact that my son, and the children of my friends who participated in the research, had died. I didn't want an honours degree in losing a child." '

The needs of parents at different times as either users or providers of services, or both at the same time, may be difficult to accommodate. As some parents find new ways of relocating their grief, a natural development may well be to move away from their resource base, while others need to maintain the same relationship to core services and contacts for many years. Perhaps this tension reflects the variety of ways in which parents forge 'continuing bonds' with children beyond death (*see* Chapter 2). In spite of these difficulties, the benefits of bereaved parents and professional helpers working co-operatively are enormous and well worth striving for. The Centre was founded on the principle that both can learn from each other and give to each other. Training offers the ideal forum for this

two-way process: staff can train parents as telephone helpline befrienders; while the experience of parents can provide valuable input
to training programmes for professionals.

The way forward

How can support services for those affected by the death of a child
be improved? Specifically, the trend appears to be towards more
inclusive family work, rather than splitting off mothers, fathers and
siblings artificially. This approach makes a lot of sense but requires
flexible and well-staffed resources. The support resources available
to a bereaved family, and to their carers, all too often seem to be a
random affair, depending on where people live. Comprehensive
systems like the Alder Centre are probably only practicable in association with a children's hospital or hospice (*see* Appendix B). Those
living in a sparsely populated rural area have a slim chance of finding a support group within easy travelling distance. On the other
hand, everyone has access to primary healthcare services and, through
them, should have access to regional and national services.

Health visitors are well placed to provide such frontline support
to families. A study conducted by Ann Dent in 1996 showed that
families are particularly vulnerable to isolation when the death of a
child is sudden and unexpected (Dent, 1996). Following this study,
interventions were devised to empower health visitors in their
support of 167 suddenly bereaved families over a two-year period in
the South and West of England. At the end of this time a follow-up
study, the results of which have yet to be published, showed significant improvement in the way families felt supported. It is interesting to note that these families felt better supported informally,
via friends and neighbours, as well as formally, through the help of
professionals such as the health visitor. Could this finding point to
nationally heightened sensitivity following Dunblane and the death
of Princess Diana?

There is a clear case for some means of auditing and co-ordinating
bereavement support services, working towards a standard provision

of care. The National Association of Bereavement Services has already done much to address this need. A Childhood Bereavement Group will conduct an audit on services for children, and regional groups have been set up to network and develop local services. On a practical level, there is still more to be done in regard to agreeing hospital protocols in the event of a child's death, leading on to procedures for liaison with community services after the death.

The usual expectation of a bereavement support agency is that bereaved parents themselves make contact, or that a third party referral is received by a concerned professional, friend or relative. Yet it is well known that the bereavement experience leaves some parents paralysed by shock, floating in a limbo of grief that renders them incapable of asking for help. Agoraphobic responses are common and members of minority groups are naturally reluctant to use mainstream services. All these factors beg the question whether support services should initiate contact, or whether this would amount to an invasion of privacy. The Kinder–Mourn Project in North Carolina, USA, is a community support agency modelled on The Compassionate Friends, who will *initiate* contact with bereaved parents brought to their attention by anyone concerned for their welfare. Home visits as early as the day of the funeral point the way towards informal parent support groups led by trained facilitators. In our more conservative British society, such proactive outreach is a less familiar concept; but arguably there is much to be achieved by support agencies reaching out to those who are unable to ask for help themselves. It is hoped that this book will give confidence to professionals to co-ordinate and advertise existing resources, and to experiment with more proactive means of support.

The guidelines offered here aim to encourage the faint-hearted as well as the visionary, and to affirm the good practice of those already engaged in providing bereavement services. Support is a two-way process. Families want information, choices and understanding.

Professional carers need assurance that they *can* and *do* help by providing information and choices, and above all by being available to accompany the family on their journey through grief.

References

Dent A (1996) A study of bereavement care after a sudden and unexpected death. *Archives of Disease in Childhood.* **74**(6): 522–6.

Stewart J (1991) *Guidelines for Setting-up a Bereavement Counselling or Support Service.* National Association of Bereavement Services, London.

Appendix A
Useful contacts for support organisations

The organisations listed below are either mentioned in the text or have a concern to support bereaved families and/or health and care professionals.

Acorns Children's Hospice Trust
As well as providing home support, respite and terminal care, Acorns offers long-term bereavement support for families and a comprehensive training programme.
Acorns Selly Oak, 103 Tree Lane, Selly Oak,
Birmingham B29 6HZ
Tel: 0121 248 4850
Acorns Education & Training Unit,
8a Wake Green Road, Moseley, Birmingham B13 9EZ
Tel: 0121 248 4818; Voicemail: 0121 248 4817

ACT (**A**ssociation for **C**hildren with life-threatening or **T**erminal conditions and their families)
Umbrella organisation providing information about available services.
Orchard House, Orchard Lane, Bristol BS1 5DT
Tel: 0117 922 1556

Alder Centre
For *all* those affected by the death of a child, providing support and counselling for families, and information and training for professionals.
Royal Liverpool Children's NHS Trust,
Alder Hey, Eaton Road, Liverpool L12 2AP
Tel: 0151 252 5391

ARC (**A**nte-natal **R**esults and **C**hoices)
Information to parents and professionals and national helpline and befriending service.
  73–75 Charlotte Street, London W1P 1LB
  Tel: 020 7631 0285 (Helpline);
  020 7631 0280 (Administration)

Association for Children with Heart Disorders
Support for families with children suffering from heart disorders.
  26 Elizabeth Drive, Helmshaw, Rossendale,
  Lancashire BB4 4JB
  Tel: 01706 213632

British Association for Counselling
  1 Regent Place, Rugby CV21 2PJ
  Tel: 01788 578328

Child Death Helpline
For all those affected by the death of a child.
  Available every evening 7pm to 10pm and
  Monday, Wednesday and Friday mornings from 10am to 1pm.
  Freephone: 0800 282986

Compassionate Friends
Nationwide self-help organisation for bereaved parents and their families; resource library; advice leaflets; group and telephone support.
  53 North Street, Bristol BS3 1EN
  Tel: 0117 953 9639

Cruse Bereavement Care
Bereavement care provided by trained counsellors, plus advice and information on practical problems and befriending.
  Cruse House, 126 Sheen Road,
  Richmond, Surrey TW9 1UR
  Tel: 020 8940 4818

Cystic Fibrosis Trust
Research, support and education.
11 London Road, Bromley, Kent BR1 1BY
Tel: 020 8464 7211

Foundation for the Study of Infant Deaths
Research, support, information and good practice guidelines.
14 Halkin Street, London SW1X 7DP
Tel: 020 7235 0965; 24-hour helpline: 020 7235 1721

Great Ormond Street Helpline
Available every evening 7pm to 10pm and
Monday, Wednesday and Friday mornings 10am to 1pm.
Freephone: 0800 282986

Hawthorn House
For any adult affected by the death of a child, providing counselling, telephone counselling, befriending for parents, support groups, information and library.
Yorkhill NHS Trust, Glasgow G3 8SJ
Tel: 0141 201 9257

ISIDA (Irish Sudden Infant Death Association)
Carmichael House, 4 North Brunswick Street, Dublin 7
Tel: (outside Ireland) (00) 3531 873 2711
Available Monday to Friday 9am to 12.45pm

Laura Centre
For *anyone* affected by the death of a child, providing professional counselling support and supervision.
4 Tower Street, Leicester LE1 6WS
Tel: 0116 254 4341

Macmillan Cancer Relief
Funds Macmillan nurses to give advice and support for cancer patients and their families.
>Anchor House, 15/19 Britten Street, London SW3 3TZ
>Tel: 020 7351 7811

Miscarriage Association
Provides support and information on pregnancy loss.
>c/o Clayton Hospital, Northgate, Wakefield,
>West Yorkshire WF1 3JS
>Tel: 01924 200799

NABS (National Association of Bereavement Services)
Referral agency and training information.
>20 Norton Folgate, London E1 6DB
>Tel: 020 7247 0617

NASS (National Association for Staff Support within the healthcare services)
>9 Caradon Close, Woking, Surrey GU21 3DU
>Tel: 01483 771599

SANDS (Stillbirth and Neonatal Death Society)
Support, information and guidelines.
>28 Portland Place, London W1N 4DE
>Tel: 020 7436 7940
>SANDS Helpline Tel: 020 7436 5881

Sargent Cancer Care for Children
Assisting all young people under 21 with any form of cancer.
>Griffin House, 161 Hammersmith Road,
>London W6 8SG
>Tel: 020 7565 5100

Scottish Cot Death Trust
Research, support, information and good practice guidelines.
   Royal Hospital for Sick Children, Yorkhill, Glasgow G3 8SJ
   Tel: 0141 357 3946

Sunrise
Offering support to all those affected by the death of a child, and to
children bereaved of a parent.
   West Midlands Child Bereavement Centre,
   83 Stirling Road, Edgbaston,
   Birmingham B16 9BD
   Tel: 0121 454 1705

TAMBA (**T**wins **A**nd **M**ultiple **B**irths **A**ssociation)
Aims to provide information and mutual support networks for
families of twins, triplets and more, highlighting their unique needs
to all involved in their care.
   Harnott House, 309 Chester Road,
   Little Sutton, Ellesmere Port CH66 1QQ
   Tel: 0151 348 0020 (Administration);
   National Helpline: 0870 121 4000;
   TAMBA Twinline: 01732 868000
   (weekdays 7pm–11pm; weekends 10am–11pm)

Winston's Wish (a grief support programme for children)
Offers a range of services to bereaved families, including 'Camp
Winston' experiences.
   Gloucestershire Royal Hospital,
   Great Western Road, Gloucester GL1 3NN
   Tel: 01452 394377
   email: info@winstonswish.org.uk;
   website: www.winstonswish.org.uk

Yorkhill Family Bereavement Service
A newly formed charity which will develop and extend the work of Hawthorn House. Plans include the provision of support for children affected by death.

c/o Yorkhill NHS Trust, Glasgow G3 8SJ
Tel: 0141 201 9257

Appendix B
Children's hospices

Acorns Children's Hospice
John L Overton, 8A Wake Green Road, Moseley, Birmingham B13 9EZ

Brian House
Dr David Cooper, Low Moor Road, Bispham, Blackpool, Lancashire FY2 0BG

*CHASE (Children's Hospice Service)
Tim Edge, 147 High Street, Godalming, Surrey GU7 1AF

*Chestnut Tree House, St Barnabas Hospice
Robin Fanshaw, Columbia Drive, Worthing, West Sussex BN13 2QF

Children's Hospice Association Scotland
John Rea, 18 Hanover Street, Edinburgh EH2 2EN

Children's Hospice South West
Mandy Robbins, Redlands Road, Fremington, Barnstaple, North Devon EX31 2PZ

*Chin-Up
Bill Sturrock, PO Box 18, Gosforth, Newcastle-upon-Tyne NE13 6YZ

Claire House
Malcolm Beard, Clatterbridge Road, Bebington, Wirral L63 4JD

Demelza House
Wendy Ely, Rook Lane, Bobbing, Sittingbourne, Kent ME9 8DZ

Derian House
Trevor Briggs, Chancery Road, Astley Village, Chorley, Lancashire PR7 1DH

East Anglia's Children's Hospices
Graham Collins, Church Lane, Milton, Cambridge, Cambridgeshire CB4 6AB

Francis House
Sister Aloysius, 390 Parrswood Road, East Didsbury, Manchester M20 5NA

*Haven House
Ivan King, 201A Cranbrook Road, Ilford, Essex IG1 4TD

Helen House
37 Leopold Street, Cowley, Oxford, Oxon OX4 1QT

Hope House
David Featherstone, Nant Lane, Morda, Oswestry, Shropshire SY10 9BX

Iain Rennie Hospice At Home
Noel Ratcliffe, The Cedar Barn, Cedar Avenue, Hazlemere, High Wycombe, Buckinghamshire HP15 7DW

James House Hospice Trust
Robin Gooch, Highbank House, Burwash Road, Broak Oak Heathfield, East Sussex TN21 8XG

*Keech Cottage
Mike Keel, Great Bramingham Lane, Luton, Bedfordshire LU3 3NT

Little Haven
Diana Causton, Daws Heath Road, Thundersley, Benfleet, Essex SS7 2LH

Martin House
Lenore J Hill, Grove Road, Clifford, Wetherby LS23 6TX

Naomi House
Jean Miles, Stockbridge Road, Sutton Scotney, Winchester, Hampshire SO21 3JE

***Northern Ireland Hospice Children's Service**
Tom Hill, 525 Antrim Road, Belfast, Northern Ireland BT15 3BS

***Phoenix Lodge**
David King, 11 Winchester Circle, Kingston, Milton Keynes MK10 0BA

Rachel House
Agnes Malone, 18 Hanover Street, Edinburgh EH2 2EN

Rainbows Children's Hospice
Harry Moore, Lark Rise, off Hazel Road, Loughborough, Leicestershire LE11 2HS

***Richard House Trust**
Heather Richardson, St Marks Church & Community Centre, Tollgate Road, Beckton, London E6 4YA

***Shooting Star Trust**
Tina Littleboy, 17 The High Street, Whitton, Middlesex TW2 7LA

***St Oswalds Hospice**
Nikki Wilkinson, Regent Avenue, Gosforth, Newcastle-upon-Tyne NE3 1EE

The Butterwick Children's Hospice
David Luke, Middlefield Road, Stockton-on-Tees TS19 8XN

*The Donna Louise Trust
David E Platt, Highfields, Parkwood Drive, Baldwins Gate, Newcastle-under-Lyme, Staffordshire ST5 5EU

Ty Hafan Children's Hospice
Dominic Jenkins, Hamard House, Cardiff Road, Barry, Vale of Glamorgan CF63 2BE

*In planning or construction stages as at the end of 1999.

Appendix C
Useful resources for working with children and families

Resource manuals

Bayliss J (1996) *Understanding Loss and Grief.* National Extension College.
> Training pack for helping and caring professions.
> Includes exercises correlated with NVQ tasks. Photocopiable.

CRUSE *Supporting Bereaved Children and Families.*
> A training manual.

Fabry L (1995) *Death and Bereavement.* The Chalkface Project.
> Photocopiable resource pack aimed at PSE or Religious Studies teachers.
> Written by Fabry in consultation with Margaret Rogers and Valerie Mandelson.

Kohner N and Leftwich A (1995) *Pregnancy Loss and the Death of a Baby* (training pack). National Extension College.
> Supports updated SANDS guidelines for professionals.

Machin L (1993) *Working with Young People in Loss Situations.* Pavilion.
> Offers practical material, including picture triggers and worksheets which can be photocopied for direct work with children.

Ward B and Associates (1992) *Good Grief: exploring feelings, loss and death. Vol 1: Under 11s. Vol 2: Over 11s and adults.* Jessica Kingsley.
> A curriculum pack of varied resources for both teachers and students.

Winston's Wish
> Produces a range of activity sheets for working with grieving children, and useful guidelines for teachers in responding to a school-related death. *See* Appendix A for address.

Videos

On The Death of a Child: a portrait of family grief (named after this book) 20 mins
> Addresses different aspects of family grief, with anecdotes and commentary. Accompanying learning pack includes useful discussion points and references.

Produced by ACORNS Children's Hospice Trust, Education & Training Unit, 8a Wake Green Road, Moseley, Birmingham B13 9EZ Tel: 0121 248 4818; Website: www.acorns.org.uk

That Morning I Went to School 12 mins
> Shows children of different ages talking about their own experiences of bereavement, their reactions and needs.

Available from Sue Smith, Social Work Dept, Northampton General Hospital, Northampton NN1 5BD.

Giving Sorrow Words 37 mins
> Useful for school staff training or individual teachers. Deals with breaking the news of a death and helping children return to school after bereavement.

Available from Video Inset, PO Box 197, Cardiff CF5 2WF

Games

Board game *All About Me* produced by Peta Hemmings and available from Barnados.
> Useful resource for adults working with primary age children.

The Grief Game produced by Yvonne Searle and Isabelle Streng, published by Jessica Kingsley.

Books for adults

Brown E (1999) *Loss, Change and Grief: an educational perspective.* David Fulton, London.

Buckman R (1992) *How to Break Bad News: a guide for healthcare professionals.* Papermac, London.

Cathcart F (1994) *Understanding Death and Dying* (booklets for carers, families, professionals). British Institute of Learning Disabilities, Kidderminster.

Downey A (1990) *Dear Stephen* (re suicide of son). Arthur James, London.

Dwivedi KN (ed) (1993) *Groupwork with Children and Adolescents: a handbook.* Jessica Kingsley, London.

Dyregrov A (1991) *Grief in Children: a handbook for adults.* Jessica Kingsley, London.

Fabian A (1988) *The Daniel Diary* (shows how young children mourn). Grafton Books, London.

Fitzgerald H (1992) *The Grieving Child: a patient's guide.* Simon and Schuster, London.

FSID (**F**oundation for the **S**tudy of **I**nfant **D**eath) produces a range of information and advice booklets for different family members and professionals. *See* Appendix A for address

Grollman EA (1990) *Talking About Death.* Beacon, Boston.

Jewett C (1984) *Helping Children Cope with Separation and Loss.* Batsford, London.

Johnson J (1984) *Suicide of a Child.* Centering Corporation, USA.

Leaman O (1995) *Death and Loss: compassionate approaches in the classroom.* Cassell, London.

Lendrum S and Syme G (1992) *Gift of Tears.* Routledge, London.

Mallon B (1998) *Helping Children to Manage Loss.* Jessica Kingsley, London.

Pennells M and Smith S (ed) (1995) *Interventions with Bereaved Children.* Jessica Kingsley, London.

Pincus L (1976) *Death and The Family.* Faber & Faber, London.

Shawe M (ed) (1992) *Enduring, Sharing, Loving.* Darton, Longman & Todd, London.

Smith S (1999) *The Forgotten Mourners: guidelines for working with bereaved children* (2e). Jessica Kingsley, London.

Turner M (1998) *Talking with Children and Young People about Death and Dying: a workbook.* Jessica Kingsley, London.

Wells R (1988) *Helping Children Cope with Grief.* Sheldon Press, London.

Wilkinson T (1991) *The Death of a Child: a book for families.* Julia MacRae Books, London.

Winston's Wish *Supporting a Child who is Bereaved Through Suicide.*

NB: Smallwood Publishing Group offers a range of useful booklets relating to miscarriage, the death of a baby or older child. For parents, grandparents, children and professionals.
Tel: 01304 226 800. Email: sales@smallwood.co.uk

Books for younger children

Brown LK and Brown M (1996) *When Dinosaurs Die: a guide to understanding death.* Little Brown & Co.
A multicultural look at dying and surrounding customs.

Busaglia L (1982) *The Fall of Freddie The Leaf.* Charles Slack, USA.
Life and death allegory.

Cohn J (1987) *I Had a Friend Named Peter: talking to children about the death of a friend.* William Morrow & Co.
Betsy's friend is killed by a car.

Fitzgerald S (1998) *The Tale of Two Dolphins (when my sister died suddenly).* Brambles Press.

Harper A (1994) *Remembering Michael.* SANDS.
Baby brother dies at birth.

Heegaard M (1991) *When Someone Very Special Dies*. Woodland Press.
> For children to illustrate their own story and feelings.

Johnson J (1985) *Where's Jess?* Centering Corporation, USA.
> Death of four-year-old's sibling.

Maple M (1992) *On the Wings of a Butterfly*. Parenting Press.
> Story about a girl coping with cancer.

Nystram C (1981) *What Happens When We Die?* Moody Press.

Stickney D (1982) *Waterbugs and Dragonflies*. Mowbrays.
> An image for life and death.

Varley S (1985) *Badger's Parting Gifts*. Hodder & Stoughton.
> Remembering a loved friend.

Viorst J (1971) *The Tenth Good Thing About Barney*. Athenaum.
> How a young boy copes with death of a cat.

Williams M (1975) *The Velveteen Rabbit*. Avon Books.

Books for older children

Grollman EA (1995) *Bereaved Children and Teens*. Beacon.

Grollman S (1988) *Shira: a legacy of courage*. Doubleday.
> Coming to terms with own death and others' reactions.

Hill D (1995) *See Ya Simon*. Puffin
> A teenager's last year with a dying friend.

Hipp E (1995) *Help for the Hard Times: getting through loss*. Hazelden.
> Self-help workbook.

Hoffman A (1988) *At Risk*. GP Putnam & Sons.
> Story of 11-year-old girl with AIDS.

Kuklin S (1994) *After a Suicide: young people speak up*. GP Putnam & Sons.
> Teenagers dealing with suicide of others, including friends.

Lowry L (1993) *A Summer to Die*. Dragon
> Death of 13-year-old girl's older sister from leukaemia.

Richter E (1986) *Losing Someone You Love*. Putnam.
> Young people share experiences about death of a sibling.

Vogel IM (1986) *My Twin Sister, Erika*. Harper and Row.
> Loss of twin sister.

Windsor P (1973) *The Summer Before*. Harper and Row.
> Girl's journal about boyfriend's accidental death.

Books for learning-disabled children

Cathcart F (1994) *Understanding Death and Dying*. British Institute of Learning Disability, Kidderminster.

Morris L and Perkins G (1996) *Remembering My Brother*. A & C Black, London.

Essential references

Ayalon O and Flasher A (1993) *Chain Reaction*. Jessica Kingsley, London.

Bowlby J (1969–80) *Attachment and Loss*, Vols 1–3: *Attachment*, Vol 1, 1969; *Separation: anxiety and anger*, Vol 2, 1973; *Loss: sadness and depression*, Vol 3, 1980. Basic Books, New York.

Buckman R (1992) *How to Break Bad News: a guide for healthcare professionals*. Papermac, London.

Capewell E (1993) Critical incident management in schools: headteachers' briefing. *Croner*. **28**: 4–5 and **29**: 5–7.

Capewell E (1994) Responding to children in trauma: a systems approach for schools. *Bereavement Care*. **Spring**: 2–7.

Cheshire Country Council (1999) *Managing the Response to Critical Incidents in Schools*. CCC, Chester.

Dagwell K, Tsui E and Yule W (1993) *Effects of a Disaster on Children's Attainment*. Unpublished.

Dent A (1996) A study of bereavement care after a sudden and unexpected death. *Archives of Disease in Childhood*. **74**(6): 522–6.

Dyregrov A (1991) *Grief in Children*. Jessica Kingsley, London.

Green J (1991) Death with dignity: meeting the spiritual needs of patients in a multi-cultural society. *Nursing Times*.

Grollman EA (1990) *Talking About Death: a dialogue between parents and children*. Beacon, Boston.

Herbert M (1996) *Supporting Bereaved and Dying Children and their Parents*. The British Psychological Society, Leicester.

Hill L (ed) (1994) *Caring for Dying Children and Their Families*. Chapman & Hall, London.

Hindmarch C (1995) Secondary losses for siblings. In: *Child: care, health and development*. **21**(6): 425–31. Blackwell Science, Oxford.

Klass D, Silverman P and Nickman S (eds) (1996) *Continuing Bonds: new understandings of grief*. Taylor & Francis, London.

Lendrum S and Syme G (1992) *Gift of Tears*. Routledge, London.

McEwan Y (1997) A challenge to the counselling culture. *Nursing Standard*. **12**(2).

Neuberger J (1987) *Caring For Dying People of Different Faiths.* Austen Cornish, London.

O'Hara DM, Taylor R and Simpson K (1994) Critical incident stress debriefing: bereavement support in schools. Developing a role for an LEA educational psychology service. *Educational Psychology in Practice.* **10**(1): 27–34.

Parkes CM (1972) *Bereavement: studies of grief in adult life.* Pelican, Harmondsworth.

Stewart J (1991) *Guidelines for Setting-up a Bereavement Service.* National Association of Bereavement Services, London.

Stroebe M, Stroebe W and Hansson R (1993) *Handbook of Bereavement.* CUP, Cambridge.

Turner M (1998) *Talking with Children and Young People about Death and Dying.* Jessica Kingsley, London.

Winnicott D (1971) *Playing and Reality.* Tavistock, London.

Worden JW (1991) *Grief Counselling and Grief Therapy* (2e). Routledge, London.

Yule W and Gold A (1993) *Wise Before The Event: coping with crises in schools.* Gulbenkian Foundation, London.

Further reading

Balk D (1990) The self-concept of bereaved adolescents: sibling death and its aftermath. *Journal of Adolescent Research.* **5**(1).

Barnard P, Morland I and Nagy J (1999) *Children, Bereavement and Trauma: Nurturing Resilience.* Jessica Kingsley, London.

Bertman SL (1991) *Facing Death: images, insights and interventions.* Hemisphere Publishing Corporation.

Birenbaum L, Robinson M, Phillips D *et al.* (1989–90) The response of children to the dying and death of a sibling. *Omega.* **20**(3).

Black D and Urbanowicz MA (1987) Family intervention with bereaved children. *Journal of Child Psychology and Psychiatry.* **28**: 467–76.

Bluebond-Langner M (1978) *The Private Worlds of Dying Children.* Princeton University Press, Princeton.

Bluebond-Langner M (1995) *Worlds of dying children and their well siblings.* In: K Doka (ed) *Children Mourning, Mourning Children.* Hospice Association of America, Washington.

Bowlby J (1979) *The Making and Breaking of Affectionate Bonds.* Tavistock, London.

Bowlby J (1991) *Attachment and Loss*, Vol 1(2e). Penguin, Harmondsworth.

Brooks B and Siegel P (1996) *The Scared Child: helping kids overcome traumatic events.* John Wiley & Sons, Chichester.

Brown E (1999) *Loss, Change and Grief: an educational perspective.* David Fulton Publishers, London.

Buckman R (1988) *I Don't Know What to Say: how to help and support someone who is dying.* Papermac, London.

Capewell E (1994) *Systems for Managing Crisis Incidents in Schools.* Capewell, London.

Cook B and Phillips S (1988) *Loss and Bereavement.* Austen Cornish, London.

Cooper D (1992) Long-term grief. In: *Death and Dying.* Open University Press, Buckingham.

Couldrick A (1991) *Grief and Bereavement: understanding children.* Sobell Publications, Oxford.

Doka K (ed) (1993) *Children Mourning, Mourning Children.* Hospice Association of America, Washington.

Donnelly KF (1988) *Recovering From The Loss of a Sibling.* Dodd Mead, New York.

Duffy W (1995) *Children and Bereavement.* National Society/Church House Publishing, London.

Dwivedi KN (ed) (1993) *Groupwork with Children and Adolescents: a handbook.* Jessica Kingsley, London.

Dyregrov A and Mathieson S (1987) Anxiety and vulnerability in parents following the death of an infant. *Scandinavian Journal of Psychology.* **28.**

Farrant A (1998) *Sibling Bereavement: helping children cope with loss.* Cassell, London.

Finlay I and Dallimore D (1991) Your child is dead. *BMJ.* **302.**

Gatliffe ED (1988) *Death in the Classroom: a resource book for teachers and others.* Epworth Press, London.

Gullo S (1985) *Death and Children.* Dobbs Ferry, New York.

Hawkins P and Shohet R (1989) *Supervision in the Helping Professions.* Open University Press, Buckingham.

Hawton K (1986) *Suicide and Attempted Suicide Among Children.* Sage, London.

Herbert M (1996) *PTSD in Children.* BPS Books, London.

Hodgkinson P and Stewart M (1991) *Coping with Catastrophe: a handbook of disaster management.* Routledge, London.

Hogan N and Greenfield D (1991) Adolescent sibling bereavement. *Journal of Adolescent Research.* **6**(1): 108.

Hornby G (1995) *Working with Parents of Children with Special Needs.* Cassell, London.

James IA (1995) Helping people with learning difficulties to cope with bereavement. *British Journal of Learning Disabilities.* **23.**

Jewett C (1984) *Helping Children Cope With Separation and Loss.* Batsford, London.

Johnson J (1984) *Suicide of a Child.* Centering Corporation, USA.

Judd D (1990) *Give Sorrow Words: working with a dying child.* Free Association Books, London.

Kinchin D (1998) *Post Traumatic Stress Disorder: the invisible injury.* Success Unlimited, Wantage.

Knapp RJ (1986) *Beyond Endurance: when a child dies.* Schocken, New York.

Knight B (1983) *Sudden Death in Infancy.* Faber & Faber, London.

Kohner N and Henley A (1991) *When a Baby Dies*. Stillbirth and Neonatal Death Society, London.

Kubler-Ross E (1970) *On Death and Dying*. Tavistock Press, London.

Kubler-Ross E (1983) *On Children And Death*. Macmillan, London.

Lamberti J (1993) Model of family grief assessment and treatment. *Death Studies*. **17**.

Lang A and Gottlieb L (1993) Parental grief reactions and marital intimacy following infant death. *Death Studies*. **17**.

Leaman O (1995) *Death and Loss: compassionate approaches in the classroom*. Cassell, London.

Littlewood J (1992) *Aspects of Grief*. Routledge, London.

Mallon B (1998) *Helping Children to Manage Loss*. Jessica Kingsley, London.

McCollum A (1975) *The Chronically Ill Child: a guide for parents and professionals*. Yale University Press, New Haven.

Mearns D and Thorne B (1988) *Person-Centred Counselling in Action*. Sage, London.

Moddia B (1992) Grief reactions and learning disabilities. *Nursing Standard*. **9**(33).

Oakley A *et al.* (1984) *Miscarriage*. Fontana, London.

Parkes CM, Relf M and Couldrick A (1996) *Counselling in Terminal Care and Bereavement*. British Psychological Society, London.

Parkes CM and Weiss RS (1983) *Recovery from Bereavement*. Basic, New York.

Pennells M and Smith S (1995) *The Forgotten Mourners: guidelines for working with bereaved children*. Jessica Kingsley, London.

Pettle MSA and Lansdown RG (1986) Adjustment to death of a sibling. *Archives of Disease of Childhood*. **61**: 278–83.

Pincus L (1976) *Death and The Family*. Faber & Faber, London.

Rando TA (1983) An investigation of grief and adaption in parents whose children have died from cancer. *Journal of Pediatric Psychology*. **8**: 3–20.

Rando TA (1986) *Parental Loss of a Child*. Research Press, Champaign, II.

Raphael B (1984) *The Anatomy of Bereavement: A handbook for the caring professions*. Unwin Hyman, London.

Raphael B (1986) *When Disaster Strikes: a handbook for the caring professions*. Unwin Hayman, London.

Sanders CM (1979–80) A comparison of adult bereavement in the death of a spouse, child and parent. *Omega*. **10**(4): 303–23.

Sanders P (1993) *A Complete Guide to Using Counselling Skills on the Telephone.* PCCS Books, Manchester.

Segal R (1984) Helping children express grief through symbolic communication. *Social Casework: Journal of Contemporary Social Work.* Family Service, USA.

Shawe M (ed) (1992) *Enduring, Sharing, Loving.* Darton, Longman & Todd, London.

Smith S and Pennells M (1995) *Interventions with Bereaved Children.* Jessica Kingsley, London.

Speck P (1978) *Loss and Grief in Medicine.* Bailliere Tindall, London.

Spinetta JJ (1974) The dying child's awareness of death: a review. *Psychological Bulletin.* **81**.

Staudacher C (1988) *Beyond Grief.* Souvenir Press, London.

Staudacher C (1991) *Men & Grief.* Souvenir Press, London.

Stedeford A (1984) *Facing Death: patients, families and professionals.* Heinemann, Oxford.

Tatelbaum J (1981) *The Courage to Grieve.* Heinemann, Oxford.

Taylor Warmbrod M (1986) Counselling bereaved children: stages in the process. *Social Casework: USA Journal of Contemporary Social Work.* Family Service, USA.

Vachon M (1981) *Occupational Stress in the Care of The Critically Ill, The Dying and The Bereaved.* Hemisphere, Washington DC.

Walter T (1996) A new model of grief bereavement and biography. *Mortality.* **1**.

Ward B *et al.* (1992) *Good Grief: exploring feelings, loss and death (i over elevens and adults; ii under elevens)* (2e). Jessica Kingsley, London.

Wells R (1988) *Helping Children Cope with Grief.* Sheldon Press, London.

Wilkinson T (1991) *The Death of a Child: a book for families.* Julia MacRae Books, London.

Zaiger N (1986) Women and bereavement. *Women & Therapy.* **4**: 1985–6.

Index

Aberfan 14–15
abortion *see* termination
abused children
    ambulance personnel 67
    social workers 96
access to child's body 126
accidental death 10
    case study 12–13
    denial 10–11
    evidence 10–11
    incidence 4, 6
    legal proceedings 11–12
    professional roles
        ambulance personnel 66
        GPs 74
        nurses 86–7
Acorns Children's Hospice 215
Acorns Children's Hospice Trust 209
Acquired Immune Deficiency
        Syndrome (AIDS), death from
        30–2
ACT 209
action plans for schools 187–8
acute illness, death from 23
    health visitors 80
    see also meningitis; viral infections,
        death from
advice, giving 124
advocacy role, social workers
        95, 96
age of child
    characteristics of child death 5
    cot death 8

grief and mourning 50–1
    and incidence of death 2
age of parent 50
age of sibling 55–6, 136–7
agoraphobia 167, 207
AIDS, death from 30–2
Alder Centre 177, 204–6, 209
ambulance personnel
    concerns 67
    function 66
    good practice 67–8
    involvement 66
    suicide cases 69
American Indians 59–60
anniversaries 61, 132
    health visitors 81
Ante-natal Results and Choices
        (ARC) 210
anxiety 39
    siblings 56, 138
ARC 210
Association for Children with Heart
        Disorders 25, 210
Association for Children with life-
        threatening or Terminal
        conditions and their families
        (ACT) 209
attending 111
Attneave, Caroline 181–3
awareness 110–11

bad news *see* breaking bad news
baptism 68, 70

Batten's disease 26
BD8 form 125
befriending 155–6, 158
    preparation 156–7
    when? 157
    who? 157
benefits, families receiving 128
bereavement
    definition 35
    see also grief and mourning,
        features of
bereavement counselling *see*
        counselling, bereavement
birth certificate 125
birthdays 61, 132
bombings 15
Book of Remembrance 62
books
    for adults 221–2
    for children
        learning-disabled 224
        older 223
        younger 222–3
breaking bad news 116–17
    how? 118–19
    parents' experiences 119–20
    when? 117
    where? 118
    by whom? 117–18
    why? 117
breakthrough phase, response
        to crisis model 182
Brian House 215
British Association for Counselling
        210
    Directory of Counsellors and
        Therapists 167
burial 127
Butterwick Children's Hospice, The
        218

cancers 21
    case study 21–3
Candle Service 62
care issues 32
'cervical incompetence' term 16
chaplains
    concerns 69
    function 68
    good practice 69–70
    involvement 68
characteristics of child death 5–6
    congenital conditions, death from
        23–6
    illness, death from 21–3
    prenatal and perinatal loss 16–21
    socially difficult deaths 27–32
    sudden and accidental deaths
        7–15
CHASE 215
Chestnut Tree House, St Barnabas
        Hospice 215
Child Death Helpline 210
child psychologists 167–8
Children's Hospice Association
        Scotland 215
Children's Hospice Service (CHASE)
        215
Children's Hospice South West 215
Chin-Up 215
Christmas 61
chronic grief 39, 40
Claire House 215
clergy
    concerns 69
    function 68–9
    good practice 69–70
    involvement 68
clichés, avoiding 141
clinical psychologists 167–8
closed groups 172

colleges 28
commemoration of child 61
community paediatric nurses
        87
Compassionate Friends, The 46–7,
        155, 170, 210
compensation 12
complicated grief 38–40
confidentiality 102
    clergy 69
    police 92
    teachers 99
congenital conditions
    death from
        incidence 4, 6
        see also cystic fibrosis;
            heart deformities;
            neurodegenerative disorders
    risk of 18
consultants *see* hospital doctors
continuing bonds
    parents 43–4, 45, 205
    siblings 57
co-ordinated approach, support
        services 204–6
    the way forward 206–7
coroner
    accidental death 11, 12
    cot death 8
    funeral arrangements 60
    legal 'ownership' of child
        124, 125
    post-mortem 126
    stillbirth 19
    suicide 28
cot death 7
    age and circumstances 8
    case study 9–10
    incidence 7–8
    legal procedures 8–9

professional roles
    ambulance personnel 66
    GPs 77
    midwives 88
    nurses 86–7
    police 91
counselling
    bereavement 76, 158
        availability 165–6
        indicators for 166
        principles 42
        purpose 158–9
        referrals for 166
        specialism 163–4
        tasks 159–60
        when? 161–3
        where? 164–5
    pre-abortion 18
    for professionals
        nurses 87
        police 93
    schools 189, 194
    by social workers 95
    supervision 106
    see also psychological support;
        psychotherapy
counsellors
    concerns 71–2
    function 71
    good practice 72–3
    involvement 70–1
    role 160–1
cremation 127
criminal proceedings 11–12, 91
Cruse Bereavement Care 210
cystic fibrosis 23–4
Cystic Fibrosis Trust 211

deaf people 124
debriefing 193–4

delayed grief 38
Demelza House 216
denial
    accidental death 10–11
    complicated grief 38, 39
    malignant disease, death from 21
    suicide 28
depression 39, 168, 182
Derian House 216
disaster 14–15
    schools 180–1, 185
disposal form 125
distorted bereavement 38
Docklands bomb 15
doctors *see* general practitioners;
        hospital doctors
Donna Louise Trust, The 218
drawing and painting 114, 163
drug misuse, death from 29–30
    incidence 4
Dunblane 14, 185, 188, 189
Dyregrov, Atle 186, 192, 193
dystrophies 26

early miscarriage 16
East Anglia Children's Hospices
        216
educative aspects of supervision 107,
        108
elation phase, response to crisis model
        182
emergency procedures and intensive
        care 120
    identified person 121
    practicalities 123
    protocol 121
    resuscitation 122
    teamwork 121
empathy 103
enduring grief *see* continuing bonds

ethical issues
    hospital doctors 84
    suicide risk assessment 134
euphemisms, avoiding 103, 118
    with siblings 141
evidence 10–11
exhaustion/elation phase, response to
        crisis model 182
experience, and bereavement theory
        33–5
experts, lack of 105

family
    first visit to 129–30, 155
        clarity 131
        honesty and genuineness
            131
        preparation 130
        realism 130
    involvement 105
    school 191
    support 153, 206
        befriending 155–8
        counselling 158–67
        groups 169–72
        practical 153–5
        psychiatry 168–9
        psychology 167–8
        social activities 172–3
    see also father; mother; parents;
        siblings
family grave 127
family therapy 168
fantasy v. reality 104–5
    siblings 137
fathers
    grief and mourning 50
        marriage/partnership, effect
            on 52
        parenting role 52

midwives 89
see also parents
firefighters 91
fostering 32
Foundation for the Study of Infant
        Deaths 155, 211
Francis House 216
Freddie the dolphin 173
Freud, Sigmund 35
funeral 59–60
    attending the 128
        foster-parents 32
        professionals 79, 129
        siblings 57, 58, 60, 128–9
    clergy 68, 69
    expenses 128
    miscarriage 16, 17
    school 191
funeral directors
    concerns 74
    function 73
    good practice 74
    involvement 73

games 220
garden of remembrance, visiting the
        61
gender factors
    cot death 8
    incidence of death 5
geneograms 115, 163
general practitioners (GPs)
    Community Health Council
        recommendations
        78–9
    concerns 76–7
    counselling referral 162
    function 75–6
    good practice 77–8
    informed of death 124

involvement 74–5
    practical support 155
genuineness 131
grandparents
    grief and mourning 53–4
    health visitors 81
    miscarriage 17
grave
    family 127
    visiting the 61, 127
Great Ormond Street Helpline 211
grief and mourning, features of
    bereavement theory, development
        35–42
    definitions 35
    grandparents 53–4
    new understandings 42–9
    parents 49–53
    rituals 58–62
    siblings 54–8, 136–8
    starting from experience 33–5
groups *see* support groups and
        organisations

Haddington, Janet 11
Hansson, Robert 42
Haven House 216
Hawthorn House 211
headstone, placing the 61
head teachers 99, 195
health visitors
    concerns 80–1
    family support 206
    function 80
    good practice 81–2
    involvement 79
    practical support 155
heart deformities 24
    case study 25
Helen House 216

helping strategies 112–13
  drawing 114
  geneogram 115
  linking 113
  prompts 113
  rituals 114
  scrapbooks 114–15
  writing 114
helplines, telephone 189–90
  see also support groups and
    organisations, contact details
Hillsborough 14, 185
Hindus
  burial or cremation 127
  mourning rituals 59, 60–1
  post-death rituals 126
  post-mortems 126
HIV/AIDS, death from 30–2
holidays 173
honesty 131
  with siblings 142, 175
Hope House 216
hospices 215–18
hospital doctors
  concerns 84
  function 82–3
  good practice 84–5
  involvement 82
Human Immunodeficiency Virus
    (HIV)/AIDS, death from 30–2
Hungerford 185

Iain Rennie Hospice at Home 216
identified person, emergency
    treatment and intensive care
    121
illness, death from
  incidence 4, 6
  professional roles
    GPs 74–5

health visitors 79
  hospital doctors 82
  schools, support for 184–5
  see also acute illness, death from;
      malignant disease, death from
incidence of child death 1–2, 5–6
  AIDS/HIV 30, 31
  cot death 7
  miscarriage 16
Income Support 128
Indians, American 59–60
information, giving 124
  to siblings 137, 142
    about the death 143–6
    about murder or suicide 146–9
    by parents 174–5
inhibited grief 38
inquest
  accidental death 11, 12, 13
  stillbirth 19
  suicide 28, 29
insanity, fear of 161
intensive care *see* emergency
      procedures and intensive
      care
involvement, being clear about
    101–2, 131
involving siblings 137
Irish Sudden Infant Death Association
    (ISIDA) 211
Islam *see* Muslims
isolation, social 28

James House Hospice Trust 216
Japan 43
Jews
  burial or cremation 127
  mourning rituals 59, 60
  post-death rituals 126
Jupiter sea disaster 15, 180–1

Keech Cottage 216
Kinder–Mourn Project 207
Kingfisher Project 176–7

language difficulties 124
late miscarriage 16
Laura Centre 204, 211
learning-disabled children, books for
       224
led groups 171
legal procedures 124–5
    accidental death 11–12
    cot death 8–9
    disaster 14
    mourning ritual 59
    murder 27
    stillbirth 19
leukaemia 21
life support, withdrawal of 122
linking 113
listening 111, 112
    to children 135
    importance of 101
Little Haven 217
Liverpool Children's Project 177
Lockerbie 14, 189
low-weight babies 8

Macmillan Cancer Relief 212
Macmillan nurses 21
malignant disease, death from 21
    case study, 21–3
managerial aspects of supervision
       107, 108
Manchester bomb 15
manuals 219
Marchioness, sinking of 11, 15
marriage, effects of child death on
       52–3
Martin House 217

media coverage
    accidental death 12, 13
    murder 27
    school 192
mementoes 61, 113, 163
memorial ceremonies 61, 62
meningitis 23, 190
midwives
    concerns 89
    function 88–9
    good practice 89–90
    involvement 88
miscarriage 16–17
    case study 17
    midwives 88
Miscarriage Association 212
mobilisation phase, response to crisis
       model 182
mothers
    cot death 8
    grief and mourning 50
        marriage/partnership, effect on
           52
        parenting role 51
    midwives 88, 89
    neonatal death 20
    termination 18, 19
    see also parents
mourning
    definition 35
    see also grief and mourning,
        features of
murder 27
    incidence 4
    telling children about 146–8
Muslims
    burial 127
    mourning rituals 59, 60
    post-death rituals 126
    post-mortems 126

NABS 207, 212
name, using the dead child's
102, 132
Naomi House 217
NASS 212
natal death *see* miscarriage; neonatal
death; stillbirth; sudden
infant death syndrome;
termination
National Association for Staff Support
within the healthcare services
(NASS) 212
National Association of Bereavement
Services (NABS) 207, 212
need, identifying the 199
support groups 201
neonatal death 20–1
birth certificate 125
grief and mourning 50
incidence 4, 6
see also perinatal loss
neurodegenerative disorders, death
from 26
normalisation 49
Northern Ireland, bombings 15
Northern Ireland Hospice Children
Service 217
nurses
concerns 86–7
function 86
good practice 87–8
involvement 86

Ojibway tribes 59–60
Omagh 15
open groups 171–2
orthodox Jews
burial or cremation 127
mourning rituals 59, 60
post-death rituals 126

paediatricians *see* hospital doctors
painting and drawing 114, 163
panic attacks 39, 167
paramedics 29
see also ambulance personnel
parents 49–50
age of child 50–1
age of parent 50
effect of child death 51
on other children 54–5, 174–6,
178–9
marriage/partnership, effects of
death on 52–3
role 51–2
taken on by grandparents 54
partnership, effects of child death on
52–3
perinatal loss
midwives 88
mourning rituals 59
see also neonatal death; stillbirth
phobias 39, 167, 207
Phoenix Lodge 217
photographs 61, 113, 163
miscarriage 17
'placental insufficiency' term 16
platitudes, avoiding 102–3, 131
befrienders 157
with siblings 141
polarisation phase, response to crisis
model 182
police
accidental death 11–12
concerns 91–2
cot death 8, 91
function 91
good practice 92–3
involvement 91
murder 27
suicide 28–9

post-modernist view of grief 42
post-mortem
    coroner's legal 'ownership' of child
        124
    funeral arrangements 60
    sudden/unknown causes of death
        11, 125–6
        cot death 8, 9
post-traumatic stress disorder (PTSD)
        15, 190, 194
practical support 153–5
predictable grief reactions 37–8
prenatal loss *see* miscarriage; stillbirth;
        termination
preterm babies
    cot death 8
    grief and mourning 50
primary care team 75
    see also general practitioners
procurator fiscal 8
protocol, emergency procedures and
        intensive care 121
psychiatry 168–9
psychological support
    family 167–8
    school 188–9
        advice and guidance 194–6
        common needs 191–2
        common reactions 190
        levels of support 192–4
psychotherapy 166–7
    supervision 106
    see also counselling

questionnaire, resources 115

Rachel House 217
Rainbows Children's Hospice
        217
reality v. fantasy 104–5

Reduce the Risk campaign
        104–5
registrars of births, marriages and
        deaths 124–5
    concerns 94
    function 93
    good practice 94–5
    involvement 93
    stillbirth 19
registration of death 124–5
    mourning rituals 59
    stillbirth 19
religion
    burial or cremation 127
    mourning rituals 58–9, 60–1, 62
    post-death rituals 126
    post-mortem 126
    see also clergy
resolution of grief 41–2, 46–7
resource manuals 219
resources
    questionnaire 115
    sufficiency of 199
respite care 26
responsibilities, clarifying 124
resting place of child before funeral
        126
resuscitation 122
retribalisation phase, response to
        crisis model 182
Richard House Trust 217
rituals, mourning 58, 114, 126
    after the funeral 60–2
    counselling 164
    funeral *see* funeral
    Japan 43
    at time of death 58–9
road traffic accidents (RTAs), death
        from 10
    incidence 4

legal procedures 12
nurses 86–7
roles, clarifying 124

Samaritans, The 155
SANDS 19, 212
Sargent Cancer Care for Children 212
Sargent cancer care workers 21, 22
schools
  effects of child death 180–4
  HIV/AIDS sufferers 32
  informing children of the death
    144–5
  murder or suicide, telling children
    about 28, 146–9
  planning and preparation 184–8
  psychological support 188–96
  see also teachers
Scottish Cot Death Trust 155, 213
scrapbooks 114–15
secondary losses for siblings 137,
  174
seeing the dead child 104
self-harm 132–3
  see also suicidal thoughts and
    attempts
self-help groups 170–1
sentences for causing accidental death
  12
shadow grief 41–2
Shooting Star Trust 217
siblings
  books for 222–4
  cot death 9–10
  emergency procedures and
    intensive care 122
  funeral 60, 128–9
  grief and mourning 54–5, 136–8
    ages and stages 55–6, 136–7
    common anxieties 56

enduring grief 57
  helping 57
  worsening 58
guidelines for talking with 135–6
  death, telling them of the 143–6
  dos and don'ts 149–50
  first principles 139–42
  murder or suicide, telling them
    of the 146–9
  terminal illness 142–3
imagination 104–5
miscarriage 17
overprotection by parents 23
parenting role 51
professional roles
  GPs 76, 78
  health visitors 81
  teachers 98
seeing the dead child 104
support 173–4
  advice for parents 174–6
  innovative groupwork and
    projects 176–9
  practical 154
  psychological 167–8
  school 98, 192
  social activities 173
SIDS see sudden infant death
  syndrome
signers 124
skills 111
  attending 111
  listening 112
social activities 172–3
Social Fund 128
socially difficult deaths 27
  grieving process 40
  incidence 4, 6
  see also AIDS, death from; care
    issues; fostering; murder;

substance misuse, death from;
    suicide
social workers
  concerns 96
  functions 95–6
  good practice 96–7
  involvement 95
  practical support 155
socioeconomic factors, cot death 8
spontaneous abortion *see* miscarriage
St Barnabas Hospice, Chestnut Tree
    House 215
stillbirth 16, 19–20
  funeral 128
  incidence 4, 6
  midwives 88, 90
  see also perinatal loss
Stillbirth and Neonatal Death Society
    (SANDS) 19, 212
St Oswald's Hospice 217
stressful situations 16
  after the death 123–8
  anniversaries 132
  breaking bad news 116–20
  emergency procedures and
      intensive care 120–3
  family visit, first 129–31
  funeral, attending the 128–9
  suicide risk assessment 132–4
substance misuse, death from 4, 29–30
sudden death
  after the death 123
  cot death 7–10
  disaster 14–15
  guidelines 125–6
  incidence 4, 6
  professional roles
    ambulance personnel 66
    GPs 77–8
    hospital doctors 82–3

schools, support for 185–6
  see also accidental death
sudden infant death syndrome (SIDS)
    7
  health visitors 80
  incidence 4
suicidal thoughts and attempt
  of disaster survivors 15
  of family members 40
    on anniversaries 132
    counselling 161–2
    risk assessment 132–4
  of suicide victims 28
suicide 27–8
  case study 28–9
  incidence 4
  teacher's role 98
  telling children about 146–7,
      148–9
Sunrise 204, 213
supervision systems 106–7, 134
  counsellors 72
  functions 107–8
  health visitors 80, 81
  importance 107
  social workers 96
  sources 109
support groups and organisations
    169–70
  contact details 209–14
  led 171
  open or closed 171–2
  self-help 170–1
  siblings 176–9
  starting 200
    calling a meeting 201–2
    delivery 203
    evaluation 203–4
    identifying the need 201
    planning 202–3

supportive aspects of supervision
107, 108
support networks 46
  for professionals 105–6, 134,
    146
    see also counselling, for
      professionals; supervision
      systems
  siblings 57
  suicide 28
support services 198
  co-ordinated approach 204–7
  core conditions 199–200
  starting a support group 200–4

TAMBA 213
teachers
  concerns 98
  effects of child death 180, 183
  function 97–8
  good practice 98–9
  involvement 97
  planning and preparation 185
  psychological support 192
  siblings 98, 192
  see also schools
teamwork, emergency procedures and
  intensive care 121
telephone helplines 189–90
  see also support groups and
    organisations, contact details
terminal illness
  breaking bad news 118
  schools, support for 184–5
  siblings 142–3
termination 18
  medically advised 18–19
  requested 18

The Butterwick Children's Hospice
  218
The Compassionate Friends (TCF)
  46–7, 155, 170, 210
The Donna Louise Trust 218
The Samaritans 155
Towyn floods 185
training 109–10
  awareness 110–11
translators 124
truthfulness *see* honesty
twins 8, 20, 89
Twins and Multiple Births
  Association (TAMBA) 213
Ty Hafan Children's Hospice 218

uniqueness of bereavement 103–4,
  157
unknown cause of death 125

videos 220
viral infections, death from 23
  meningitis 23, 190

When a baby dies 8–9
whirlpool of grief model 47–8
Winston's Wish 177–8, 213
Wise Before the Event 185–6, 187
Worden, William
  complicated grief 39
  mourning phases and tasks 36–7,
    43–4
  predictable grief reactions 37
writing 114, 163

Yorkhill Family Bereavement Service
  214
Yule, William 136, 181, 186